D0605486

FAVOURITE
BALTI
and Indian recipes

FAVOURITE
BALTI
and Indian recipes

Sabiha Khokhar ❖ Lali Nayar ❖ Geeta Samtani

MEREHURST

Published 1997 by Merehurst Ltd
Ferry House, 51–57 Lacy Road, Putney London SW15 1PR

Edited by **Val Barrett**
Designed by **Sara Kidd**
Photography by **Steve Baxter,**
except pages 46–52 and 94–97 by **Alan Marsh**
Styling by **Jane McLeish,**
except pages 46–52 and 94–97 by **Suzy Gittings;**
pages 66–69, 90–93, 112–125 and 142–153 by **Marian Price**
Food for Photography by **Annie L Nichols,**
except pages 46–52 and 94–97 by **Valerie Berry**
Cover Illustration by **Ken Cox**

Colour separation by P&W Graphics Pte Ltd. Singapore
Printed by New Interlitho Italia SpA

CONTENTS

INTRODUCTION

Baltistan is not an easy place to visit, situated as it is in the midst of the Karakorams, Hindu Kush and Himalayas. It is in the north-east corner of Pakistan, just north of Indian-held Kashmir (disputed territories), to the east is Ladakh, to the west is Gilgit and to the north is China. Sometimes known as 'Little Tibet' and the 'land where mountains meet', it was part of the ancient Silk Trade route and once belonged to Tibet but when the Moguls came to Kashmir they conquered Baltistan as well.

There are three types of cooking in Baltistan, typical Balti foods, Punjabi foods brought in by travellers and visitors and some Kashmiri foods. It is said that many traditional Balti dishes are dying out as the people copy dishes from other regions.

Beef is the most commonly eaten meat and tends to be rather tough. When a cow is slaughtered the meat is stored on top of the houses, in direct sun, where it is dried. It is then used, as and when required, by first soaking in warm water for 30 minutes, then boiling in the same water for 30 minutes. The water is discarded and the meat is then cooked in various ways. This beef is very tough as the animals are often quite old, so it takes a very long time to cook.

Chicken is very expensive in Baltistan and is rare to find in the winter. Although an expensive luxury for the people, it is still their favourite meat and is cooked for guests and at feasts or to provide nourishment if someone is ill. For all the chicken dishes, chicken on the bone is used because the resulting dish will have a rich taste and sucking on the chicken bones, after eating the meat, is part of the pleasure. Of course you may substitute boneless chicken in any of the recipes, but take care to reduce the cooking time and dry off excess liquid before adding the chicken.

Although Baltistan is very far from the sea and so has no sea-water fish, it does have a good supply of fish from the mighty River Indus, many other little rivers and large and small lakes. The fish are similar to those found in the cold European waters, so you can use fish that are readily available here in the recipes.

In Baltistan, as in the rest of Pakistan, the Muslims eat as much meat as they can find but due to the shortage of cows, goats and chickens in the region, meat is very expensive and in the winter it is very scarce. This leads the majority of the Balti people to eat a lot of potatoes, dhals, chick-peas and vegetables. Some vegetables, such as wild carrots, turnips, peas, spinach, coriander and beans, are grown in the region. Others such as cauliflower, aubergines, okra and dhals, are brought in from the lowlands. Vegetables are rarely flown in but usually arrive after long journeys in trucks and buses en route from Rawalpindi to Skardu. In the winter road transport gets risky and dangerous, so sometimes fresh produce does not get through. The Baltis are very aware of this problem and overcome it by drying all their vegetables in the sun during the summer. They, like any other people who cook a lot of curry, are very fond of coriander. They miss this the most in the winter, so plenty of it is dried in the summer. Sun-dried vegetables are soaked in water for about 30 minutes and then cooked as for fresh. Some of these stored items actually save time and effort when cooking, for example sun-dried tomatoes are simply crushed into a powder and just sprinkled into the dish that is being cooked.

The Balti people are not really rice eaters even though their neighbours, the Kashmiris, introduced them to rice and it is grown around Baltistan. The majority of main course Balti dishes are eaten without rice and only with nans, chapattis, tandoori roti or on their own. Rice is cooked mainly for festive occasions and weddings.

In Baltistan, pickles, chutneys and raitas are eaten in very small quantities with main dishes and dry starters, to provide extra flavour. Plenty of mango, lime and wild carrot pickles are made in the summer, using mustard oil and special spices like fennel, onion seeds, fenugreek, black mustard seeds and cumin. The pickles last through the winter and they are, at the same time, sweet, sour, salty and tangy.

India, with its enormous geographical and human diversity is a wonderland of the East. Within its boundaries are many different states, which in turn have different physical, historical, social and cultural aspects. Deeply embedded in the many regions lie the variations of cooking as well as the eating habits of the people. Food, more than anything else, is a great dividing factor and a major essential in labelling the differences between the far flung regions of India.

The well-used words "variety is the spice of life" cannot ring more true than within the realms of regional Indian cuisine. It provides an astonishing mosaic of taste, texture, flavour and appearance which is vast, varied and bewildering. However, in spite of all this diversity, there is the underlying unity of a majority of the ingredients used and that forces the regions to shed their individuality to some extent and come under the blanket term of 'Indian food'. Even so, the many superb regional culinary styles have definite characteristics. A legendary one amongst them is Punjabi cuisine which has no doubt been responsible to a great extent for promoting the love of Indian food outside India.

Lying in the north-west region of India, Punjab, or the land of the five rivers, has a cuisine which over the years has been influenced by a string of invaders such as the Persians, Afghans, Greeks and Mongols. This has resulted in the cuisine now being not only rich and exotic, but robust and earthy as well. The indomitable, spirited Punjabis have acquired a reputation for being the greatest food lovers in India, whose tantalisingly, tasty and nutritious preparations are as full of zest as the people themselves. To help them further, the soil, climate and geographical position of Punjab supply rich produce and enables Punjabis to make food that can be a gastronomic discovery, especially for those who are new to Indian cuisine.

The Vale of Kashmir, often called 'The Switzerland of India', is situated in the north of the country and is enclosed on all sides by the snow-capped Himalayas. From this green and fertile land come wonderful vegetables, peaches, plums, almonds, wheat, yellow mustard and golden saffron. With these ingredients the Kashmiris skillfully prepare many mouthwatering dishes.

So if you relish good cooking why not take an adventurous dip into this book and try some of the best recipes from Baltistan, Punjab and the Vale of Kashmir.

Easy Route to Confident Balti and Indian Cooking

Most Balti and Indian recipes are very simple to prepare and need very little equipment. In fact a lot of dishes are cooked and served in one pan, called a karahi or kadhai. This is a round-bottomed pan with two handles, rather similar to a wok. It can be used for cooking and deep frying but you can use a lidded, heavy-based saucepan or frying pan instead. A griddle or tawa is the other utensil used by the Baltis and Indians, especially for cooking breads. Tawas can be bought in Indian shops or you can use a griddle or large, heavy-based frying pan. A blender or food processor is a useful item to have as it will cut down on the time spent chopping and grinding.

Special Fresh Ingredients

There are some items used for flavouring that are essential ingredients in the majority of the dishes and which are a chore to prepare every time. It is therefore a good idea to make some of these items in advance and store them so there is always some to hand.

Garam Masala

Garam masala is a mixture of dry spices which are roasted and then ground. It will keep in a closed jar for up to a month. To give the garam masala a longer shelf life, after grinding immediately cover the outside of the jar with foil. This stops light from affecting the taste of the spices and the masala should then last for up to three months. There are many versions of garam masala and we recommend you make the one below to give an authentic Balti flavour.

If you want to use shop-bought garam masala, use a well-known Indian or Pakistani brand bought from Asian grocers or a supermarket. Some own brand garam masalas contain items not recommended for use in Balti cooking.

To make Balti garam masala:
1 tablespoon coriander seeds
1 teaspoon black peppercorns
2 small sticks cinnamon
1 large brown cardamom pod (optional)
4 whole cloves
2 tablespoons cumin seeds

1. Heat a frying pan on a low heat for 5 minutes. Add the coriander, peppercorns, cinnamon, cardamom and cloves. Dry roast for 1 minute or until the mixture gives off an aroma, then add the cumin. Dry roast for 30 seconds and switch off. Remove from the heat and cool completely.
2. Grind all the spices in a coffee grinder and store in a tightly-covered jar.

To make 60g (2 oz) Indian garam masala:
22g (³/₄ oz) brown cardamoms
22g (³/₄ oz) cinnamon stick
7g (¹/₄ oz) black cumin seeds
7g (¹/₄ oz) whole cloves
10 black peppercorns
large pinch of fresh grated nutmeg

1. Shell the cardamoms.
2. In a grinder, put the cardamom seeds, cinnamon, cumin seeds, cloves, peppercorns and nutmeg. Run the machine until they blend into a fine powder..
3. Store immediately in an airtight container. It lasts well, but not indefinitely, and it is better to make it fresh in small amounts to get the best flavour.

Ground Fresh Garlic

This is used in a lot of the recipes and advance preparation will save time. It will keep in a jar for up to 10 days in the refrigerator. The mixture can be frozen in small plastic bags or in an ice cube tray and used as required. Peeling garlic is a tedious but essential task, but there are easy ways to do it, some of which are listed below. Asian grocers and supermarkets sell bottles and tubes of puréed garlic, these are expensive to buy but can be used in the recipes if you wish.

To make Ground Fresh Garlic:
250g (¹/₂ lb) garlic cloves
water

1. To peel the garlic, break up the bulbs and separate the cloves. Soak in warm water for 4 hours, or overnight, before peeling.
    Or microwave a few cloves at a time, for a few seconds to soften the skin, then peel.
    Or smash the garlic clove with the flat side of a large knife. The clove will break and the skin will come off and can easily be separated and discarded.
2. Put the peeled garlic and a little water into a blender and process until a fine paste is achieved. Alternatively use a food processor and process without adding any water until the garlic is finely chopped.
3. Put into a jar, close tightly and store in the salad drawer of the refrigerator.

Suitable for freezing.

Confident Balti and Indian Cooking

Ground Fresh Root Ginger

Again this is used in the majority of the recipes and advance preparation will save much time. It will keep in a jar for up to 10 days in the refrigerator. It can also be frozen in plastic bags or in an ice tray and the cubes used as required. Peeling ginger is not essential before using in recipes and it can be puréed to a pulp with the skin. Asian grocers and supermarkets sell bottles of puréed ginger and this can be used in the recipes if liked.

To make Ground Fresh Root Ginger:
250g (½ lb) fresh root ginger
water

1. Use a pan scourer or knife to scrape off any dirty nodes of ginger and wash the root in plenty of cold water. As it is a rhizome and grows in the earth, make sure it is cleaned very well.
2. Cut against the grain into 2.5cm (1 inch) slices. Put into a blender and process with enough water to make a fine paste. Alternatively, put into a food processor, without any water, and process until the ginger is finely chopped.
3. Put into a jar, close tightly and store in the salad drawer of the refrigerator.

Suitable for freezing.

Ground Fresh Green Chillies

Chillies can be stored whole, in a brown paper bag, in the salad drawer of the refrigerator for up to a week. Chillies have their own scale of heat of 1-10. They range from the very hot ones, which if touched will keep your hand burning for at least 4 hours, to the very mild which are just for use as a vegetable and add a green colour. Normally, the smaller the chillies the hotter they are. The seeds are always left in and therefore a small amount is enough.

To make Ground Fresh Chillies:
60g (2 oz) fresh chillies
2 tablespoons lemon juice (optional)

1. Wash the chillies in cold water and leave on the stalks.
2. Put into a food processor or blender and process until finely chopped. Add the lemon juice if you use a blender.
3. Put in a tightly-closed jar and store in the refrigerator for up to a week.

Suitable for freezing. Freeze in small amounts as this does not keep well once thawed.

Paneer (Home-made Cheese)

Paneer is home-made Indian cheese and a remarkable ingredient. It is an incredible source of protein and especially good for vegetarians. Surprisingly, it is a very easy cheese to make and needs no expertise or special equipment.

To make approx. 125-180g (4-6 oz) of paneer:

600ml (1 pint) full cream milk
1 tablespoon lemon juice or $\frac{1}{2}$ teaspoon citric acid
125ml (4 fl oz) hot water

1. Put the milk in a saucepan and bring to the boil. Stir now and then to prevent a skin forming on the top.
2. Mix the lemon juice or citric acid with the hot water. Add gradually to the milk as soon as it begins to boil, and stir gently.
3. Remove from the heat, cover and leave for about 5 minutes. The milk will then curdle and the whey will separate.
4. Strain through a muslin cloth and squeeze out all the whey. The milk mixture left in the bag is "paneer". This can be used as it is for a variety of sweet and savoury dishes, or it can be converted into a block, cut into pieces and then used.
5. To convert the paneer into a block, leave it in the muslin bag and press it down with a heavy weight for at least 2-3 hours to make a slab. This can then be cut into cubes.
6. The pieces can be used as they are, or can be deep fried to a light golden colour and then used.
7. The paneer will keep for 2-3 days in a fridge.

Mustard Oil (Sarson Ka Tel)

Kashmir is known for its wonderful fields of golden mustard. The oil is made from the mustard seeds and is pungent in its raw form. However, on heating, the pungency is eliminated and a sweet flavour remains. It is an important oil in Indian cuisine, particularly for making pickles. In Kashmir it is also used for everyday cooking. Before using mustard oil, heat it to smoking point (to eliminate the pungency), lower the heat and simmer for a few seconds. The oil is now ready for use.

Glossary

Ajowan (Ajwain or Carom Seeds): From the same family as caraway and cumin, it has a strong flavour similar to thyme. Often used in batter mixtures and coatings.

Aniseed (Saunf): Aromatic and sweet-flavoured seeds of the anise plant. Aniseed is an important spice in Kashmiri cuisine. It is used in savoury dishes and for flavouring drinks, and is also eaten after meals to aid digestion.

Asafoetida (Hing): This is the dried resinous gum of a plant grown in Afghanistan and Iran. It is used sparingly as it has a very strong flavour.

Atta: Atta is finely ground wheat flour. It is readily available in major supermarkets and Asian grocers and is sometimes called chapatti flour. It is sold in packets marked brown, medium brown or white according to the amount of wheat husk it contains.

Bhun: This is a very special process and the ultimate stage in many of the dishes. When onions, ginger, garlic and tomatoes are added to oil and cooked, they produce a lot of liquid. This excess liquid has to be dried off and the ingredients should form a fine pulp and the oil, butter or ghee should separate out – this stage is called bhun.

Cardamoms (Elaichi): They are either green or brown or sometimes white. The white variety are bleached green cardamoms. The green or white are used in sweet recipes and some special dishes like biryanis or kormas. Only the seeds are used and the skin is discarded. The large brown type is used whole, with the skin and sticky seeds, as a spice.

Cassia (Dal Chini): Sometimes known as Chinese cinnamon. This spice is very closely related to cinnamon although it is much coarser and slightly different in flavour.

Cumin (Zeera): These resemble fennel seeds. Where mentioned in the recipes use white cumin, dry roasted and cooled. Where black cumin is required it is mentioned.

Dhal: These are pulses or lentils and there are over sixty different types! The better known are listed below and are available in Indian grocery stores and large supermarkets.

Masoor dhal are split, skinless, red lentils. They are dark brown when whole but when split and the skin is removed, the colour is bright pinky orange.

Moong dhal are split, skinless, moong lentils. They are dark green when whole but once split and skinned they are yellow and oval-shaped.

Channa dhal are split, black, gram lentils. They are from the chick-pea family but are smaller and have a dark brown husk. When split and skinned they are bright yellow and resemble yellow split peas. Gram flour (besan) is made from these lentils.

Maash dhal are split, skinless, Urad lentils. The skins are black and these lentils come whole, split or polished and in the latter form the colour is off-white.

Kabli channa are chick-peas. They are round and beige in colour and need to be soaked before using.

Dhum: A special term used mainly for slow cooking. It occurs by tightly closing the pan and sealing it either with a tight lid, a layer of foil or a mixture of flour and water placed around the lid, so all the steam remains inside the cooking pot and cooks the ingredients slowly but surely. For example, the final cooking of rice on a very low heat, tightly covered for 10-15 minutes without stirring, is the dhum stage.

Fenugreek (Methray): This comes as seeds and as fresh leaves. The seeds are mainly used for pickling and the leaves are used as a vegetable.

Food colour (Khaanwala Rang): Yellow and red food colouring powders can be bought in Indian grocery stores. There is also a tomato-coloured powder that gives a true 'tandoori' look to dishes.

Ghee: Pure ghee is made by clarifying butter. Vegetable ghee is also readily available and is a healthier substitute with a slightly different flavour and texture, but oil can be used if preferred.

Karahi: This is the special utensil in which most of the dishes are prepared and it is then sometimes used for serving. The karahi is very similar to the wok and is usually made of cast iron which retains heat well and saves the food from sticking to the bottom.

Kulfi-de-Saanche: Cone-shaped aluminium moulds about 7.5-10cm (3-4 inches) long. Used for freezing kulfi (Indian ice-cream). You can use small yogurt cartons instead.

Mango, dried (Amchoor): Raw mangos are dried and used as a souring agent in cooking. Can be bought whole or powdered.

Masala: This is a mix of various ingredients which can be wet or dry. For example onions, ginger, garlic and tomatoes cooked in oil is a wet masala, whereas garam masala is a dry spice mixture.

Mooli (Daikon, White Radish): This is from the radish family but has a white skin and white interior. The flavour is strong and biting and the texture is crunchy.

Pomegranate Seeds (Anardana): Dried seeds of a small and sour variety of the pomegranate fruit; they add a tangy flavour.

Red Chilli Powder: This is made from dried chillies. Don't be tempted to grind them at home because they give off a very strong, suffocating, pungent aroma. Red chilli powder is used in almost all recipes and the amount used will make the dish hot or mild. It is best to follow exact measurements for the first attempt and then adjust according to personal taste. Always try and buy from an Asian grocer the variety marked Red Chilli Powder, mild, medium or hot. Choose according to your preference. Whilst it is available at some supermarkets, check to make sure it does not contain other ingredients.

Rose essence (Kewda): Colourless liquid distilled from rose petals and used for flavouring desserts. When water is added it is called Rosewater (Gulabjal).

Silver leaves: Edible silver beaten into extremely thin and light sheets. Used for decoration it is available at selected Asian grocers.

Tamarind (Imli): Dried pods of the tamarind tree. The flesh and juice is very sour and it is sold in compressed blocks or paste form which keep for a very long time.

Tarka: This is a special process achieved by heating the oil or ghee in a small heavy frying pan until it is very hot and then adding ginger, garlic, onion or whole spices. The mixture is left to sizzle for 30-50 seconds and then poured directly over the food in the serving dish. Used mainly when cooking dhals or some vegetable dishes.

LAMB AND BEEF DISHES

Yellow Balti Meat

SERVES 6-8

*T*he Baltis traditionally use beef in this recipe. Serve it in a large karahi and eat it with lots of large nans to dip into the gravy. Here lamb has been substituted to reduce the cooking time.

1kg (2 lb) leg of lamb with
   bone, cut into 10cm (4 inch)
   pieces, (ask your butcher to
   do this for you)
1 teaspoon salt
1 tablespoon ground fresh root
   ginger
1 tablespoon ground garlic
1-2 teaspoons ground turmeric
500g (1 lb) onions, coarsely
   chopped
1 teaspoon ground fresh green
   chillies
900ml (1½ pints) water
7 tablespoons corn oil
10-12 dried plums (or 2 table
   spoons tamarind extract)
up to 1 tablespoon freshly
   ground black pepper,
   according to taste

Preparation time: 10 minutes
Cooking time: 1 hour 30 minutes

1. Put the meat into a large karahi or deep pan, add the salt, ginger, garlic, turmeric, onions, fresh chillies and water. Bring to the boil, uncovered.
2. Simmer, covered, on a low heat for 1 hour or until meat is tender. Carefully remove the meat leaving the liquid in the pan.
3. Boil the liquid rapidly to reduce to a thick gravy. Stir in the oil, then add the plums or tamarind extract and stir on low heat until oil separates from the mixture – the bhun method.
4. Add meat and cook well until the mixture has no excess liquid. Stir well, keep on very low heat tightly covered, and cook for 30 minutes. Add 2 tablespoons of water at a time, if required, to prevent the mixture from sticking to the bottom.
5. Stir in black pepper to taste and serve.

Serve in the karahi or pan with nans.

Suitable for freezing.

Fried Beef Chops
SERVES 4-6

*T*he Baltis use large beef chops, almost the size of T-bone steaks, for this dish. The dish is quite dry and it is served in the cooking pan. Everyone helps themselves to a chop straight from the pan – no need for plates! You can use lamb chops in this recipe and reduce the cooking time accordingly.

125g (4 oz) natural yogurt
1kg (2 lb) T bone steak, beef ribs or sirloin steak
1 teaspoon salt
1 tablespoon ground fresh green chillies
1 tablespoon ground fresh root ginger
600ml (1 pint) water
oil for deep frying
60g (2 oz) finely sliced onion
2 tablespoons lemon juice
1 tablespoon Balti garam masala
2 tablespoons chopped fresh coriander

Preparation time: 10 minutes plus 2-4 hours marinating
Cooking time: 2 hours

1. Put the yogurt into a piece of muslin or a clean J-Cloth, tie a knot and hang over a bowl to drain off the liquid whey. Leave to drain for 30 minutes.
2. Put the beef chops in a large bowl. Add the salt, chillies, ginger and drained yogurt. Toss well together and leave in a cool place to marinate for 2-4 hours or overnight.
3. Put the meat into a pan with the water. Cover and cook on a low heat for about 1 hour or until meat is tender. (The cooking time may be reduced if you are using very tender cuts of beef). Add more water if required.
4. When cooked, remove the lid and cook on a high heat to dry off any remaining liquid.
5. Add the oil to a karahi or deep pan and deep fry the chops, one or two at a time. Remove and keep warm.
6. Heat a large flat karahi, or frying pan, and add the onion and 1 tablespoon oil. Cook until the onions are dark brown. Sprinkle with lemon juice.
7. Pile the chops on to a serving dish, garnish with the onions, garam masala and fresh coriander and take sizzling to the table.

Serve as a starter with tomato ketchup or any chutney and a raita.

Suitable for freezing.

Lamb and Beef Dishes

Balti Tawa Lamb

SERVES 2-3

This special dish is made in some restaurants on a large griddle or tawa, 1 metre (3 feet) in diameter. Small pieces of marinated meat are cooked and placed on to the side of the tawa. A nan is soaked in water and put in the middle of the tawa with all the meat juices and masalas. The nan is then flipped over and pressed into the juices for a few seconds, to produce a soft, juicy delicious bread.

500g (1 lb) lean boneless lamb or rump steak

1 tablespoon dry roasted cumin seeds

1 teaspoon ground fresh root ginger

1 teaspoon ground garlic

1 teaspoon salt

$1/2$ teaspoon red chilli powder

3 tablespoons natural yogurt

2 tablespoons ghee or 5 tablespoons oil

125g (4 oz) chopped onions

250g (8 oz) chopped tomatoes

1 teaspoon chopped fresh green chillies

3 tablespoons chopped fresh coriander

1 teaspoon Balti garam masala

Preparation time: 10 minutes plus marinating time
Cooking time: 35 minutes

1. Cut the meat into 5 x 2.5cm (2 x 1 inch) strips, 5mm ($1/4$ inch) thick. Put into a bowl. Bruise the cumin by rubbing with your palms and add to the meat. Add the ginger, garlic, salt, red chilli powder and yogurt to the meat. Marinate for 2-4 hours or overnight. This will help to reduce cooking time and flavour the meat.
2. Add ghee or oil to a large heavy-based griddle/tawa, karahi or frying pan, add the onions and fry until they are transparent. Add the tomatoes and stir. Add the marinated mixture and cook, covered, on a low heat for 30 minutes or until the meat is tender. Stir the mixture from time to time to stop it from sticking, add a tablespoon of water at a time if required. Uncover and dry off any excess liquid and the oil should separate from the mixture.
3. Stir in the fresh chillies, fresh coriander and garam masala.

Serve with nans.

Suitable for freezing.

Balti Tawa Lamb and Balti Muthi Kebabs (p.20)

Balti Muthi Kebabs
SERVES 4

*M*uthi kebabs is a popular dish in many homes because it is cheap and filling. *Muthi means fist in Urdu. The mince is shaped by gently crushing in the fist hence the name – muthi. Alternatively the mince can be shaped into rounds or long ovals.*

For Muthis:
500g (1 lb) lamb or beef mince
250g (8 oz) finely chopped or
    grated onion
1 tablespoon crushed fresh root
    ginger
2 tablespoons chopped fresh
    coriander
1 teaspoon chopped fresh green
    chillies
1 teaspoon salt
1 egg

For Balti Gravy:
4 tablespoons cooking oil
125g (4 oz) finely sliced onion
500g (1 lb) chopped fresh
    tomatoes or 400 g (14 oz)
    can chopped tomatoes
2 tablespoons lemon juice
$\frac{1}{2}$ teaspoon red chilli powder
$\frac{1}{2}$ teaspoon salt
$\frac{1}{4}$ teaspoon turmeric
1 tablespoon Balti garam
    masala
3 tablespoons chopped fresh
    coriander

Preparation time: 20 minutes
Cooking time: 35 minutes

1. Put the mince in a large bowl and add the remaining ingredients. Mix well and divide the mixture into 10-12 portions. With wetted palms shape each portion into a small round ball and hold in the middle of the palm. Make a fist thereby crushing the mince gently to form an oblong shape with finger marks, to make muthis. Make all the kebabs and place on a large flat plate.
2. Put all the kebabs into a large karahi or a non-stick frying pan. Cook without any fat, uncovered, on medium heat, until all liquid evaporates and the kebabs are cooked. Alternatively cook under a pre-heated grill for 5 minutes each side or until brown. Remove the kebabs and keep warm.
3. To make the gravy, put the oil in a karahi and fry the onions until transparent. Add the tomatoes, lemon juice, red chilli powder, salt and turmeric.
4. Cook, uncovered, on medium heat for 5 minutes or until excess liquid has evaporated. When a thick gravy remains, add the kebabs and mix once with a wooden spoon. Cook on a low heat for 5 minutes. If the mixture sticks to the bottom of the karahi, add 2 tablespoon water and stir.
5. Remove from heat and sprinkle with garam masala and fresh coriander. Keep covered for 5 minutes before serving.

Serve with chapattis or nans.

Suitable for freezing, cooked or uncooked.

Chapli Kebab

SERVES 5-6

Chapli kebabs are common all over Baltistan, but recipes vary. This recipe has a Peshawari influence. The Chapli kebab literally translates into 'slipper' kebab, so named due to the large 20cm (8 inch) size and leathery appearance of the kebab. The maize meal is an important ingredient and is readily available from all major supermarkets or Asian grocers. If not available substitute semolina. Chapli Kebabs can be served in baps, with all the trimmings, for a Balti Burger!

250g (8 oz) onions
125g (4 oz) tomatoes
5cm (2 inch) fresh root ginger
1 teaspoon ground fresh chillies
500g (1 lb) lamb or beef mince
1-2 teaspoons salt
$\frac{1}{2}$ teaspoon red chilli powder
2 teaspoons Balti garam masala
1 teaspoon coriander seeds, coarsely crushed
1 teaspoon cumin seeds, crushed
2 tablespoons crushed anardana (dried pomegranate seeds – omit if not available)
125g (4 oz) chopped fresh coriander
2 tablespoons ground maize meal
oil for shallow frying

Preparation time: 15 minutes
Cooking time: 30 minutes

1. Put the onions, tomatoes, ginger and green chillies into a food processor. Blend until they are finely chopped.
2. Put the mince into the processor bowl, add the salt, red chilli powder, garam masala, crushed coriander, cumin, anardana if used, fresh coriander, and maize meal. Process for 3-4 minutes or until a fine mixture is formed. Remove to a large bowl.
3. Divide the mixture into 12-14 portions. Take one portion, wet the palms of your hands and make into a burger about 10cm (4 inch) in diameter.
4. Heat the oil in a non-stick pan on very low heat, until oil is hot. Gently lower the burger into the oil and fry on a low heat for 3-5 minutes on each side or until cooked through. Put into a covered dish. Fry all the burgers in the same way.
5. Just prior to serving, reheat 2 or 3 burgers at a time, on high heat in a dry, non-stick frying pan or griddle for 30 seconds on either side, until brown and crisp.

Serve with a fresh green salad and a dash of lemon juice.

Suitable for freezing.

Gosht Boti Kebab
SERVES 6

It is not really known where this dish originated, but the Baltis believe they invented it. However it is very popular in Karachi and they insist they exported it to Baltistan. It is commonly made in restaurants or by roadside hawkers on barbecues, but you can get very good results using a grill.

1kg (2 lb) rump steak or bone-less leg of lamb, sliced into thin strips, 10cm (4 inch) by 4cm (2 inch) and 5mm ($^1/_4$ inch) thick (approx)
1 teaspoon ground fresh root ginger
1 teaspoon ground fresh garlic
1 teaspoon ground fresh green chillies
125g (4 oz) onion, grated or finely chopped in a food processor
1 tablespoon Balti garam masala
1 teaspoon ground mace
$^1/_2$ teaspoon ground nutmeg
1 teaspoon ground cassia
2 teaspoons meat tenderiser or 60g (2 oz) finely grated raw paw paw
8 tablespoons low fat natural yogurt
2 teaspoons salt
1 teaspoon red chilli powder
4 tablespoons corn oil

Preparation time: 20 minutes, plus 5-7 hours marinating and draining
Cooking time: 30 minutes

1. Put the meat in a bowl. Add all the other ingredients and marinate for 3-4 hours.
2. Put the whole mixture into a J-cloth, tie a strong knot and hang to drain, over a bowl, for 2-3 hours.
3. Remove the strips of meat from the mixture and lay out on the grill rack. Cook under a preheated grill on full power for 5-7 minutes on each side or until meat turns brown and is cooked.
Alternatively, thread onto skewers and cook on a barbecue.

Serve with any chutney.

Suitable for freezing.

Gosht Boti Kebab and Balti Chops (p.24)

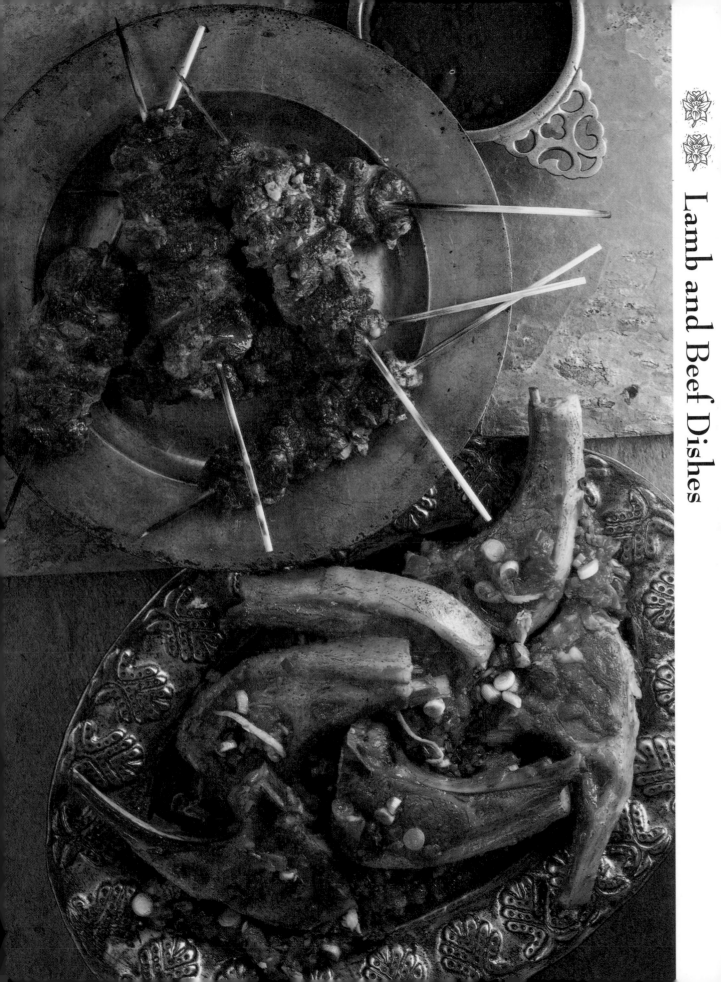

Balti Chops
(Balti Chaamp)
SERVES 3

*A*ny meat or poultry can be used in this recipe – chicken is good – and the bones are left in to add extra flavour to the gravy.

6 tablespoons oil
1 teaspoon ground fresh garlic
1 teaspoon ground fresh root
   ginger
500g (1 lb) fresh chopped
   tomatoes
500g (1 lb) lamb chops, neck of
   lamb or other meat, cut into
   2.5cm (1 inch) pieces
1 teaspoon salt
½ teaspoon red chilli powder
½ teaspoon ground turmeric
600ml (1 pint) water
2 tablespoons grated fresh root
   ginger
30g (1 oz) butter
4 tablespoons chopped fresh
   coriander
1 teaspoon chopped fresh green
   chillies
 60g (2 oz) spring onions, sliced
   (optional)

Preparation time: 10 minutes
Cooking time: 1 hour

1. Put the oil in a karahi or frying pan, add the ground garlic and ginger and fry until they are golden brown. Stir in the tomatoes.
2. Add the chops, salt, red chilli powder, turmeric and water. Stir well and cook, covered, on low heat for 50 minutes or until meat is tender. Add more water, if required, to fully cook the meat. Once the meat is cooked, dry off any excess liquid by cooking, uncovered, on high heat. When the mixture starts to thicken, turn heat to low and keep stirring until the oil separates out - this is the bhun method. Some thick gravy should remain.
3. Add the grated ginger and butter. Stir and cook, uncovered, on a low heat for 5 minutes or until the butter separates out.
4. Add the fresh coriander, fresh chillies and spring onions. Stir once and remove from the heat. Do not cook further as the onions should remain crunchy.

Serve with chapattis or nans.

Suitable for freezing.

Salt Meat
(Namkeen Gosht)
SERVES 4-6

*I*n Baltistan, once the meat is cooked it is put into a very large, round, silver dish and placed in the middle of the room. All the guests surround the dish and break off bits of the meat, dip it in Lassi flavoured with mint and chew on it. They don't rush the meal; it could take up to three hours of chatting and eating which helps to pass the time during the long winter months.

1kg (2 lb) leg of lamb with
   bone, cut into large 10cm
   (4 inch) pieces
1 tablespoon salt
1 tablespoon ground cassia or
   cinnamon
1 tablespoon ground fresh root
   ginger
1 tablespoon ground fresh
   garlic
600ml (1 pint) water
10 tablespoons vegetable oil or
   3 tablespoons ghee
350g (12 oz) finely sliced
   onions

Preparation time: 10 minutes
Cooking time: 1 hour 15 minutes

1. Put the meat in a karahi or deep frying pan. Add the salt, cassia or cinnamon, ginger, garlic and water. Bring to the boil and simmer, covered, on low heat for 1 hour, or until the meat is tender. You may need to add more water to cook the meat. Alternatively cook meat in a pressure cooker to save time.
2. Dry off all excess liquid by cooking, uncovered, on full heat and then remove from the heat.
3. Heat the oil in a frying pan or karahi. Add the onions and fry until they are dark brown. Either discard onions or use in a rice recipe.
4. Pour the hot flavoured oil from the frying pan onto the meat in the karahi. This is a process known as tarka.

Serve with Mint Lassi. Place the Lassi in small individual bowls around the table for dipping the meat or serve with tomato ketchup or any chutney.

Suitable for freezing.

Balti Green Lamb
(Haray Masala Wala Gosht)
SERVES 3-4

*T*he name of this dish is very apt as there is no red chilli powder or turmeric, but there is plenty of coriander and raw green tomatoes to give it a green colour.

500g (1 lb) leg or shoulder of lamb with bone, cut into 2.5-5cm (1-2 inch) pieces
1 teaspoon salt
1 tablespoon ground fresh green chillies
1 tablespoon ground fresh root ginger
1 teaspoon ground fresh garlic
250g (8 oz) coarsely chopped onion
600ml-1.15 litres (1-2 pints) water
10cm (4 inch) stick cinnamon
10 black peppercorns
1 tablespoon whole white cumin seeds
1 teaspoon whole coriander seeds
6 whole cloves
250g (8 oz) crushed green unripe tomatoes
6 tablespoons oil
8 tablespoons chopped fresh coriander

Preparation time: 10 minutes
Cooking time: 1 hour 20 minutes

1. Put the meat into a pan and add the salt, fresh chillies, ginger, garlic, onions and water. Bring to the boil. Simmer, covered, on low heat for 50 minutes or until meat is tender, adding more water if required. Alternatively use a pressure cooker to cook the meat.
2. Add the cinnamon, peppercorns, cumin, coriander and cloves. Cook, uncovered, and dry off all excess liquid by cooking, uncovered, on high heat. Add the tomatoes and oil and cook, uncovered, on medium heat for 7-10 minutes to dry off the mixture. Turn to a low heat setting and stir from time to time until oil separates from the mixture – the bhun method.
3. Add the coriander and simmer, tightly covered, on very low heat for 10 minutes.

Serve with chapattis or nans.

Suitable for freezing.

Balti Green Lamb with chapattis

Roast Leg of Lamb
(Dhum Pukht)
SERVES 6-7

In parts of Baltistan this is made in the winter. A whole cow or goat is coated in spices, covered with edible leaves and then cooked on hot coals in a deep hole in the ground. The meat is left to cook overnight and most of the following day. Here is a version using a leg of lamb.

2.25kg (4-5 lb) leg of lamb
2 tablespoons salt
1 tablespoon dried red chillies (reduce if you prefer a mild flavour)
2 tablespoons Balti garam masala
2 tablespoons ground ginger
2 tablespoons garlic powder

Preparation time: 15 minutes plus 2-4 hours marinating
Cooking time: 2 hours 20 minutes, approx.

1. Score the leg of lamb with long slashes to a depth of 1cm ($\frac{1}{2}$ inch).
2. Put the salt, red chillies, garam masala, ginger and garlic into a bowl and mix together. Rub the mixture over the leg of lamb, taking care to rub deep into the cuts. Transfer to a roasting tin and wrap tightly with aluminium foil. Allow to marinate in a cool place, for 2-4 hours or overnight.
3. Preheat the oven to 170°C, 325°F, Gas Mark 3. Put the lamb in the oven and cook, covered, for 2 hours, (adjust according to the weight of the lamb). Uncover and cook at 200°C, 400°F, Gas Mark 6 for 10 minutes or until brown on one side. Turn the whole leg over and cook for a further 10 minutes. Place on a serving platter.
4. Transfer the liquid from the roasting tin to a pan. Leave to stand until the fat separates, then skim off and discard the fat. Boil vigorously on full heat and reduce the liquid until a thick gravy remains.

Serve the lamb with the gravy and with ketchup or any chutney.

Suitable for freezing.

Balti Lamb

SERVES 4

This recipe uses boneless lamb. If the fat on the surface of the curry is too much for your liking, just spoon off the excess and discard.

2 tablespoons oil
1 tablespoon grated fresh garlic
500g (1 lb) boneless lamb, cut into 4cm (1½ inch) cubes
600ml (1 pint) water
500g (1 lb) finely chopped fresh tomatoes
1 teaspoon salt
½ teaspoon ground turmeric
1 teaspoon red chilli powder
2 tablespoons ghee or butter
2 tablespoons chopped fresh coriander
1 teaspoon Balti garam masala

Preparation time: 10 minutes
Cooking time: 40 minutes

1. Put the oil and the garlic in a large karahi or pan, and cook on a medium heat. When the garlic begins to sizzle add the meat and fry on full heat until it is browned all over. Add the water, tomatoes, salt, turmeric and chilli powder and bring to the boil. Simmer, covered, on low heat for 30 minutes or until the meat is tender. Add more water if required.
2. Stir the mixture from time to time and dry off any excess liquid that remains.
3. Add the ghee or butter and simmer, uncovered, on low heat for 10 minutes or until the fat separates from the mixture and a thick gravy remains – the bhun method.
4. Garnish with the coriander and garam masala and serve.

Serve with chapattis or nans.

Suitable for freezing.

CHICKEN
AND EGG DISHES

Balti Eggs
(Unday Ka Salun)
SERVES 2

*E*ggs, *like chickens, are a luxury to the Balti people as only the well-off can afford them. They are transported in wooden cases full of rice husk for minimal break-ages and grocery stores will sell one or more wrapped up in home-made paper bags for safe transport.*

1 tablespoon oil
$^1/_2$ teaspoon whole cumin seeds
125g (4 oz) sliced onions
1 tablespoon grated fresh root
  ginger
60g (2 oz) sliced tomatoes
salt to taste
pinch of ground turmeric
$^1/_2$ teaspoon red chilli powder
4 eggs, beaten
2 sliced fresh green chillies
  (optional)
2 tablespoons chopped fresh
  coriander

Preparation time: 10 minutes
Cooking time: 10 minutes

1. Place the oil in a karahi or non-stick pan and add the cumin. When this sizzles, add the onions and ginger and stir until onions are just softened.
2. Add the tomatoes, salt, turmeric and red chilli powder. Cook, uncovered, on a low heat for 5 minutes to dry off the liquid.
3. Add the eggs and keep stirring until the mixture coagulates. Cook, uncovered, for a further 5 minutes or until oil separates out. Remove from the heat and garnish with the fresh chillies and fresh coriander.

Serve with toasted bread, rolls, croissants or chapattis. Or serve mixed in with plain rice and accompanied with plain yogurt.

Unsuitable for freezing.

Previous pages: Chapattis (p.128), Balti Chicken Zeera (p.33) and Balti Eggs

Balti Chicken Zeera

SERVES 6-8

In Baltistan, this dish is cooked and then served in the karahi. Everyone dips in with large pieces of bread and scoops out the chicken.

4 tablespoons whole white cumin seeds

4 tablespoons vegetable or corn oil

60g (2 oz) grated or finely chopped onion

1 whole brown cardamom pod

4 whole cloves

5cm (2 inch) piece cassia bark

1 teaspoon ground fresh green chillies

1 teaspoon ground fresh root ginger

1 teaspoon ground fresh garlic

1 teaspoon salt

1 teaspoon red chilli powder (optional)

1 tablespoon ground coriander

1 kg (2 lb) boneless chicken, cut into 5cm (2 inch) pieces

2 tablespoons chopped fresh coriander

Preparation time: 20 minutes
Cooking time: 40 minutes

1. Heat a small frying pan and add the cumin seeds. Dry roast for 30-40 seconds or until the cumin gives off an aroma. Remove at once. Cool and grind coarsely in a coffee grinder. Put in a small bowl.
2. Heat the oil in a karahi or deep frying pan, add the onion and fry on high heat until brown. Add the cardamom, cloves, cassia and fresh chillies and fry the mixture on medium heat for 5 minutes or until it turns brown.
3. Add the ginger, garlic, salt, red chilli powder and coriander. Stir well over a high heat for 30-40 seconds, then simmer for 7-10 minutes or until excess liquid evaporates.
4. Add the chicken pieces and cook, uncovered, on a medium heat for 7-10 minutes or until some of the liquid evaporates and the chicken is par-cooked. Add the cumin.
5. Simmer, covered, on low heat for 10 minutes until chicken is cooked. If the mixture starts to stick, add 2 tablespoons of water at a time and mix well. If the mixture contains too much liquid, cook uncovered to allow the excess to evaporate. Stir in the fresh coriander and serve.

Serve in the karahi with chapattis, nans or tandoori chapattis and natural yogurt.

Suitable for freezing.

Balti Chicken Tikka Masala

SERVES 6-8

A *familiar and popular dish in the UK, this is a similar dish from Baltistan, where it is cooked with chicken on the bone and called Chicken Makhani.*

1-1.5 kg (2-3 lb) whole skinned
  chicken
Marinade:
6 tablespoons natural yogurt
1-2 teaspoons salt
1 teaspoon red chilli powder
2 teaspoons ground cumin
1 tablespoon ground fresh root
  ginger
2 tablespoons oil
2 tablespoons lemon juice
a pinch yellow and red food
  colour or ½ teaspoon of
  ground turmeric (optional)

For the Masala:
90g (3 oz) butter
1 tablespoon oil
180g (6 oz) chopped or grated
  onions
500g (1 lb) chopped fresh
  tomatoes or 400g (14 oz)
  can tomatoes
1 teaspoon salt
1 teaspoon red chilli powder
125ml (4 fl oz) single cream
2 tablespoons natural yogurt
4 tablespoons chopped fresh
  coriander
1 tablespoon dry roasted whole
  cumin seeds

Preparation time: 20 minutes plus 2-4 hours marinating
Cooking time: 1 hour

1. Make cuts 1cm (½ inch) deep into the chicken. Put the yogurt into a bowl. Add all the remaining marinade ingredients and mix well. Spread this over the chicken making sure it penetrates into the cuts. Leave in a cool place to marinate for 2-4 hours.
2. Preheat the oven to 200°C, 400°F, Gas Mark 6. Put the chicken, with all of the marinade, into a large roasting bag in a roasting tin. Put into the oven and cook for 50-60 minutes, or until the chicken is cooked. Turn the roasting bag over halfway during cooking.
3. Allow the chicken to cool. Cut the chicken into 5cm (2 inch) pieces, cover, and put to one side.
4. Place the butter and oil in a karahi or deep frying pan on low heat and add the onions. Fry for 3-4 minutes. Add the tomatoes, salt and red chilli powder, mix well and cook, covered, on a medium heat until the oil separates.
5. Stir in the cream and yogurt and mix well on a medium heat for 3 minutes or until mixture thickens. Gently lower the chicken pieces into the karahi. Cover and simmer on low heat for 5 minutes or until heated through.
6. Sprinkle with fresh coriander. Bruise the roasted cumin in the palm of your hand and sprinkle on to the chicken.

Serve with nans or chapattis.

Unsuitable for freezing.

Balti Chicken Tikka Masala

34

Pressed Chicken
(Dabah Murgh)
SERVES 4

*I*n Baltistan this chicken dish is sometimes served at roadside stalls. It is very tender and the taste of the garlic penetrates right through the chicken.

1 kg (2 lb) chicken, skinned
1 tablespoon coarsely ground
    dried red chillies
1 tablespoon salt
2 tablespoons coarsely ground
    garlic with skin
4 tablespoons lemon juice or 6
    tablespoons white wine
    vinegar
1 tablespoon meat tenderiser or
    2 tablespoons crushed raw
    paw paw or 2 tablespoons
    crushed melon skin
oil for deep frying
500g (1 lb) finely sliced onions
150ml (5 fl oz) vegetable oil
ground garlic mixed with a
    little water

Preparation time: 20 minutes plus 2 hours marinating
Cooking time: 1 hour 30 minutes

1. Place the chicken on a chopping board and cut through the breast up to the neck. This will help to "flatten" the chicken. Use a sharp knife to score the chicken.
2. Make a paste with the chillies, salt, garlic, lemon or vinegar and tenderiser. Spread the paste all over the chicken and leave in a cool place for 2 hours or more.
3. Put the oil in a deep karahi or frying pan. Add 2 tablespoons of onions at a time and fry until golden brown. Remove, drain and set aside.
4. Heat the measured oil in a large non-stick frying pan and gently lower the chicken into the pan. Put a heavy weight on top of the chicken to press it down into the oil (e.g. a heavy saucepan or a heavy dish). Cook on full heat, until chicken starts sizzling, then cook, covered, on a low heat for 20 minutes each side, or until the chicken is tender.
5. Heat a griddle, tawa or a non-stick frying pan. Put the chicken onto this, again with a weight on top to flatten it. Cook on very, very low heat for 15 minutes each side until dark brown. Splash the chicken with a little garlic water and serve.

Serve on a large platter garnished with the fried onions.

Suitable for freezing.

Chicken Kebabs
(Murgh Kebab)
SERVES 3-4

*I*n Baltistan these are made in some hotels and restaurants and are very expensive. Only the white meat is used in this recipe.

500g (1 lb) chicken mince or 500g (1 lb) boneless chicken breasts blended to a coarse paste in a food processor
125g (4 oz) finely chopped spring onions
1 tablespoon ground cumin
1 tablespoon Balti garam masala
1 teaspoon salt
1 tablespoon chopped fresh coriander
1 teaspoon ground fresh green chillies (optional)
1 beaten egg
4 tablespoons fine semolina
oil for shallow frying

Preparation time: 10 minutes
Cooking time: 15 minutes

1. Put the chicken mince in a large bowl. Add the onions, cumin, garam masala, salt, coriander and chillies and mix well.
2. Divide into 12 portions. Make each one into a small flat 7.5cm (3 inch) burger or a long oval kebab.
3. Dip in beaten egg, then in semolina and shallow fry until cooked through and golden brown.

Serve cold with a salad or as a hot starter.

Suitable for freezing.

Bhallay

SERVES 4-5

*O*ne of the few prominent traditional dishes in Baltistan today. It is a quite fiery and very nourishing broth and the noodles are obviously an influence from China. Locals drink dollops of it in the winter evenings for warmth.

250g (8 oz) finely chopped
  boneless chicken
250g (8 oz) chicken or lamb
  bones (optional)
2 teaspoons salt
1 teaspoon red chilli powder
125g (4 oz) whole tomatoes
1 teaspoon ground turmeric
2 teaspoons Balti garam masala
2 x 4cm (4 inch) pieces of
  cassia
4 whole cloves
1 teaspoon black peppercorns
2 litres (4 pints) water
500g (1 lb) Chinese noodles,
  thick vermicelli or small
  fresh or dried pasta

Preparation time: 10 minutes
Cooking time: 1 hour 10 minutes

1. Put the chicken and bones into a large saucepan and add the salt, red chilli powder, tomatoes, turmeric, garam masala, cassia, cloves, peppercorns and water. Bring to the boil and cook, uncovered, on medium heat for 5 minutes. Then simmer, covered, for 40 minutes or until the mixture thickens. Stir from time to time.
2. Add noodles and simmer, covered, for a further 10-15 minutes or until the noodles are cooked and very soft.

Serve piping hot in bowls to be slurped from a deep spoon.

Unsuitable for freezing.

Steam Roast Chicken (p.40) and Bhallay

Steam Roast Chicken
SERVES 4

For this recipe, chicken is marinated then fried, marinated again, then steamed. In Baltistan it is slow-cooked in a large clay pot on embers in a hole in the ground. A steel lid is placed on top and tightly sealed with a thick paste made with flour and water. The whole cooking process can take all night.

For Marinating:
1 kg (2 lb) chicken, cut into 4
  equal pieces and skinned
6 tablespoons lemon juice
4 tablespoons white wine
  vinegar
1 tablespoon salt
2 tablespoons black
  peppercorns, ground
oil for deep frying

For Steaming:
6 tablespoons natural yogurt
1 teaspoon ground turmeric
1 tablespoon Balti garam
  masala
1 teaspoon salt
1 teaspoon red chilli powder
1 tablespoon ground fresh
  green chillies
1 tablespoon ground fresh root
  ginger
1 tablespoon ground fresh
  garlic

60g (2 oz) sliced onion
1 tablespoon oil
a little lemon juice or water

Preparation time: 30 minutes plus 2 hours marinating
Cooking time: 1 hour 10 minutes

1. Wash and score chicken and drain in a colander for 20 minutes. Mix together the lemon juice, vinegar, salt and black pepper in a large bowl. Add the chicken pieces and marinate in a cool place for 2 hours or more.
2. Place the oil in a deep karahi or pan and heat. Fry the chicken pieces, one at a time, for 7-10 minutes or until chicken is almost cooked. Cool completely.
3. Put the yogurt, turmeric, garam masala, salt, red chilli powder, fresh chillies, ginger and garlic into a bowl and mix to form a paste. Spread the paste all over the chicken pieces and wrap them up in foil.
4. Place a strainer in the middle of a large pan and add enough water to come half way up the strainer. Bring water to the boil then simmer. Gently place the foil wrapped chicken on the strainer and steam for 30 minutes. Alternatively use a steamer.
5. Put the onion in a frying pan, add 1 tablespoon oil and fry the onions until brown. Carefully splash with lemon juice or water. Pile the chicken pieces onto the sizzling brown onions and serve.

Serve with chutney.

Suitable for freezing.

Chicken Kashmiri

SERVES 4-6

This recipe from Baltistan uses roasted spices blended with yogurt, which is in fact a Kashmiri influence.

1 teaspoon black cumin seeds
1 teaspoon white cumin seeds
1 tablespoon black peppercorns
4 brown cardamom pods
5cm (2 inch) piece cassia bark
1kg (2 lb) boneless chicken
6 tablespoons natural yogurt
4 tablespoons oil
6 whole cloves
2 teaspoons salt

Preparation time: 10 minutes plus 2 hours marinating
Cooking time: 20 minutes

1. In a hot frying pan, dry roast both types of cumin seeds, peppercorns, cardamoms and cassia bark for 30 seconds and grind in a coffee grinder.
2. Clean the chicken and wash in cold water. Pat dry with kitchen paper.
3. Put the yogurt in a bowl, add the freshly ground spices, oil, whole cloves and the salt and mix well.
4. Put the chicken into a karahi or deep frying pan. Add the yogurt mixture and stir with a wooden spoon until chicken pieces are coated with the mixture. Leave to marinate in a cool place for 2 hours.
5. Switch on the heat under the karahi. Cook, covered, on a medium heat for 10 minutes, then uncovered for a further 10 minutes or until chicken is tender. Stir 2 or 3 times during cooking. If any liquid remains, cook uncovered to dry off. Turn heat to lowest setting for about 7 minutes or until the oil separates out.

Serve with twists of lemon and nans or chapattis.

Suitable for freezing.

Chicken Fry With Fruit Fritters

SERVES 5-6

This is very popular with American and European tourists who visit Baltistan as it is a dish that is mild and light in spices.

For marinating:
1kg (2 lb) chicken, cut into 12 pieces
8 tablespoons lemon juice
1 teaspoon Chinese salt, (a mix of salt, pepper and five-spice powder)
2 teaspoons ground black pepper
2 tablespoons tomato ketchup
1 teaspoon salt
oil for deep frying

For the fruit fritters:
2 bananas
2 red eating apples
250g (8 oz) plain flour
1 egg
milk for batter
oil for frying

Preparation time: 20 minutes plus 30 minutes marinating
Cooking time: 45 minutes

1. Wash the chicken and drain well in a colander. Put into a deep bowl.
2. Mix together the lemon juice, Chinese salt, ground pepper, tomato ketchup and the ordinary salt. Add this mixture to the chicken in the bowl. Mix well and put aside for 30 minutes or more.
3. Put the oil in a karahi or deep frying pan and when hot, fry the chicken pieces 3 or 4 at a time for 7-10 minutes or until nearly cooked. Fry all the chicken in the same way and keep warm in a covered dish.
4. Cut the bananas lengthways once and then in half across the width. Core the apples and cut into circular slices 5mm (1/4 inch) in thickness.
5. Put the flour and egg in a bowl. Add enough milk to mix to a smooth batter.
6. Return the oil in the karahi to the heat. Dip the chicken pieces, one at a time, in the batter and gently lower into the hot oil. Fry 3 or 4 pieces at a time and when all the chicken pieces have been refried put them in a large serving dish.
7. Dip each fruit slice into the batter and deep fry until crisp and golden and place on top of the chicken pieces.

Serve with tomato ketchup.

Unsuitable for freezing.

Balti Chicken (p.44) and Chicken Fry with Fruit Fritters

Balti Chicken

SERVES 4-5

It is said that a true Balti dish does not contain onions. Well here is a true Balti Chicken recipe using onions, contrary to belief!

1kg (2 lb) chicken on the bone, cut into 5cm (2 inch) pieces

3 tablespoons oil

60g (2 oz) grated onion

1 tablespoons grated fresh garlic

750g (1½ lb) finely chopped fresh tomatoes or 500g (1 lb) chopped canned tomatoes

1 teaspoon ground turmeric

½ teaspoon red chilli powder

2 teaspoons salt

60g (2 oz) butter or 2 tablespoons ghee

1 tablespoon coarsely ground cumin

1 tablespoon coarsely ground coriander

2 tablespoons grated fresh root ginger

4 tablespoons chopped fresh coriander

2 finely sliced jalapeno peppers (optional)

1 teaspoon Balti garam masala

Preparation time: 10-12 minutes
Cooking time: 40-45 minutes

1. Wash chicken pieces with cold water and put in a colander to drain.
2. Place the oil in a karahi or deep frying pan, add the onion and garlic and stir-fry for 1 minute on a high heat. Add the tomatoes and cook, uncovered, on medium heat for 10 minutes or until the liquid is reduced.
3. Add the chicken pieces, turmeric, red chilli powder and salt. Stir well and cook, covered, on low heat for 20-25 minutes, or until chicken is tender. On medium heat, allow all excess liquid to evaporate until a thick gravy remains.
4. Add the butter or ghee, ground cumin, ground coriander, ginger and chopped coriander and simmer for 7-10 minutes or until the fat separates out. Add the sliced jalapeno peppers if desired and garnish with the garam masala.

Serve with chapattis, tandoori chapattis or nans.

Suitable for freezing.

Balti Chicken Korma

SERVES 6-8

*T*his is a dish made at weddings and festivals like Idd. Some claim it comes from the migrants of Karachi, others believe it is from the time of the Moguls and originates from the time of their reign of Kashmir. It is a very special dish and is different from the korma served in the West as it is lacking in cream, and chillies are included so it is not a mild dish.

oil for deep frying
125g (4 ozs) finely sliced onions
1 tablespoon ground fresh root ginger
1 tablespoon ground fresh garlic
1 teaspoon ground fresh green chillies (increase if desired)
1 teaspoon salt
1 teaspoon red chilli powder
$\frac{1}{2}$ teaspoon ground turmeric
4 tablespoons tomato purée
1 kg (2 lb) chicken, cut into 5cm (2 inch) pieces
400g (14 ozs) chopped fresh tomatoes or canned puréed tomatoes
7 tablespoons natural yogurt

Preparation time: 15 minutes
Cooking time: 45 minutes

1. Half fill a karahi or deep pan with oil. Heat the oil, add 2 tablespoons onions at a time and fry to a golden brown. Use a slotted spoon to remove onto kitchen paper. Fry all the onions and keep spread out so they turn crispy when they dry.

2. Leave 6 tablespoons of this oil in the karahi. Add the ginger, garlic, green chillies, salt, red chilli powder, turmeric and tomato purée and stir-fry for 1 minute on medium heat. Add the chicken pieces and fry, uncovered, on medium heat for 5-8 minutes.

3. Add the tomatoes and yogurt. Stir from time to time and cook on medium heat for 15-20 minutes or until all the excess liquid evaporates and the chicken is cooked.

4. Bruise the crisp fried onion in the palms of your hands and add to the chicken in the pan. Mix well and simmer on very, very low heat for 5-10 minutes until oil rises to the top. To eat with rice, add 300-350ml (10-12 fl ozs) boiling water, simmer on a low heat for 5 minutes. Remove from the heat and keep covered for a further 5 minutes for the fat to rise to the top, and serve.

Serve with nans or chapattis.

Suitable for freezing.

Saffron Chicken
(Kesar Murgh)
SERVES 4-6

*K*ashmir is the only place in India where saffron, the world's most expensive spice, is harvested. This simple dish glistens with a beautiful orange colour obtained from the aromatic saffron.

1kg (2-2^1/$_4$ lb) chicken
2.5cm (1 inch) piece fresh root ginger, peeled
3-4 cloves garlic, peeled
3 tablespoons butter or ghee
1 medium onion, finely chopped
2 green chillies, thinly sliced
^{1}/$_2$ teaspoon saffron, soaked in 2 tablespoons hot water
^{1}/$_2$ teaspoon ground cardamom
salt to taste
^{1}/$_2$ teaspoon freshly ground black pepper

Preparation time: 20 minutes
Cooking time: 30 minutes

1. Cut the chicken into 8-10 pieces and remove the skin.
2. Grind the ginger and garlic to a paste.
3. In a heavy-based pan melt the butter and add the onion, garlic-ginger paste and chillies and sauté until the onion becomes transparent.
4. Add the chicken pieces, stir and add the saffron water, ground cardamom and salt to taste. Mix thoroughly.
5. Cover and cook on a very low heat until the chicken is cooked and all the liquid has evaporated. This should take approximately 15-20 minutes.
6. Just before serving sprinkle the dish with freshly ground black pepper.

Serve hot with rice.

Suitable for freezing.

Badam Murgh (p.48) and Kesar Murgh

Almond Chicken
(Badam Murgh)
SERVES 4-6

S pring in Kashmir is heralded with the appearance of almond blossoms. Much of Kashmiri cooking incorporates almonds and this dish is often called 100 Almond Chicken. Fresh mint is added to the dish for extra flavour and a fresh aroma.

100 almonds approx 125g
   (4 oz), blanched
500ml (16 fl oz) natural yogurt
5-6 tablespoons ghee or oil
1kg (2-2¼ lb) chicken, cut into
   8 pieces and skinned
3 medium onions, finely sliced
6-8 cloves garlic, peeled and
   ground to a paste
2.5cm (1 inch) piece fresh root
   ginger, peeled and ground to
   a paste
8 small green cardamom pods
1 teaspoon chilli powder
½ teaspoon ground fennel
1 teaspoon black cumin
   seeds, ground
1 teaspoon ground coriander
½ teaspoon ground turmeric
4 medium tomatoes, chopped
1-2 teaspoons salt or to taste
4 tablespoons fresh mint leaves,
   chopped

Preparation time: 30 minutes
Cooking time: 45-60 minutes

1. Reserve 10 almonds. Grind the rest of the almonds with the yogurt in a blender or food processor and set aside. Slice the reserved 10 almonds and fry until golden brown and set aside.
2. Heat the ghee or oil in a heavy-based frying pan. Fry the chicken pieces until golden brown. Remove from the oil and set aside.
3. In the same pan, add the onions and fry on a low heat until golden. Do not allow to brown as this will change the colour of the sauce.
4. Add the garlic, ginger, cardamoms, chilli powder, fennel, ground black cumin seeds, coriander and turmeric and stir-fry for 2 minutes. Add the tomatoes, salt and 2 tablespoons of the mint. Cover and cook on a low heat, stirring frequently until the mixture thickens and the oil floats to the top.
5. Add the chicken pieces. Stir and add the almond-yogurt mixture. Cover and leave to simmer on a low heat until the chicken is cooked.
6. Serve garnished with the fried almonds and the remaining fresh mint.

Serve hot with rice or any Indian bread.

Suitable for freezing.

Coriander Chicken
(Dhaniwala Murgh)
SERVES 4-6

This is a colourful dish that can be made with chicken or meat. A speciality of the Wazas (Kashmiri chefs), it is served alongside lamb curry, meatball curry, cauliflower and rice at festive occasions.

1 bunch coriander leaves, about
   15g (^{1}/$_2$ oz)
1kg (2-2^1/$_4$ lb) chicken, cut
   into 8 pieces and skinned
2 brown cardamom pods
^{1}/$_2$ teaspoon ground turmeric
500ml (16 fl oz) water
4-6 tablespoons ghee or oil
2 medium onions, finely sliced
3 whole cloves
4-5 green cardamom pods,
   crushed
2.5cm (1 inch) cinnamon stick
500-750ml (16-24 fl oz) natural
   yogurt, well beaten
6-7 cloves garlic, peeled and
   ground to a paste
salt to taste
^{1}/$_2$ teaspoon freshly ground
   black pepper,

Preparation time: 30 minutes
Cooking time: 40 minutes

1. Wash and clean the coriander by removing the leaves from their stalks and chop finely.
2. Put the chicken, brown cardamoms, turmeric, and water into a pan and cook on a low heat for 20 minutes or until the chicken is tender. Remove the chicken and strain the stock. Set aside.
3. Heat the ghee or oil in a heavy-based pan, and add the onions and fry until crisp and reddish-brown in colour. Remove the onions and drain.
4. In the same oil, add the cloves, cardamom pods, cinnamon, yogurt and garlic and continue stirring on a medium heat until the sauce has thickened and the oil begins to separate out.
5. Add the boiled chicken and the salt to taste. Cook, stirring continuously until the sauce coats the chicken. Add the reserved stock. Cook, stirring from time to time, until the liquid reduces and just coats the chicken.
6. Just before serving, stir in the fried onions, ground black pepper and the fresh chopped coriander leaves.

Serve hot with rice or bread.

Suitable for freezing.

Murgh Noorjhani
SERVES 4

*T*his dish was specially made for Noorjahan, the consort of Jhangir (a renowned Moghul King). A splendid garden in Kashmir has also been named after her.

8 chicken drumsticks
6 tablespoons natural yogurt
4-6 cloves garlic, peeled and ground to a paste
2.5cm (1 inch) piece fresh root ginger, peeled and ground to a paste
4 tablespoons ghee or oil
2 medium onions, finely chopped
2 tomatoes, chopped
1 teaspoon ground cumin
2 teaspoons ground coriander
$\frac{1}{2}$ teaspoon chilli powder
$\frac{1}{2}$ teaspoon ground turmeric
2 tablespoons raisins
2 tablespoons unsalted cashew nuts, halved
salt to taste
500ml (16 fl oz) water
$\frac{1}{2}$ teaspoon Indian garam masala
1 tablespoon fresh coriander leaves, finely chopped

Preparation time: 30 minutes plus 4 hours marinating
Cooking time: 30-40 minutes

1. Skin the chicken drumsticks and prick them all over with a fork.
2. Mix the yogurt with the garlic and ginger pastes and spread over the chicken. Leave in a cool place to marinate for 4 hours.
3. Heat the ghee or oil in a heavy-based saucepan and fry the onion until light brown. Add the tomatoes, cumin, coriander, chilli powder, turmeric, raisins, and cashew nuts. Continue stir-frying until all the moisture evaporates and the oil separates out.
4. Add the chicken and salt to taste. Cook over a low heat, stirring all the time. When the mixture begins to stick and the liquid has evaporated, add the water. Cover and leave to simmer on a low heat until the chicken is cooked.
5. Sprinkle on the garam masala and coriander leaves and serve.

Serve hot with nans or chapattis.

Suitable for freezing.

Murgh Noorjhani with chapattis and tomato chutney

Chicken and Egg Dishes

Spinach Chicken
(Palag Murgh)
SERVES 4-6

*T*his dish can also be made with lamb or beef. Kashmiris are very fond of combining meat or fish with greens to create a colourful and appetising dish.

2-3 green chillies
500g (1 lb) fresh spinach,
    washed and dried
2 large onions
2.5cm (1 inch) piece fresh root
    ginger, peeled and ground to
    a paste
10-12 cloves garlic, peeled and
    ground to a paste
125ml (4 fl oz) ghee or oil
60ml (2 fl oz) milk
1kg (2-2¼ lb) chicken, cut
    into 8 pieces and skinned
½ teaspoon chilli powder
1 teaspoon Indian garam
    masala
salt to taste
3 tomatoes, finely chopped
125ml (4 fl oz) single cream

Preparation time: 45 minutes
Cooking time: 45 minutes

1. Put the green chillies and spinach into a blender or food processor and blend to a paste.
2. Separately, in a clean blender or food processor, grind the onions to a paste. Mix with the ginger and garlic pastes.
3. Heat the ghee or oil in a heavy-based pan. Add the onion, ginger and garlic pastes. Fry until pinkish-brown by adding a little milk to prevent the pastes from sticking to the bottom.
4. Add the chicken and fry for 1 minute. Add the chilli powder, garam masala, and salt to taste. Stir-fry until all the moisture evaporates and the oil separates out.
5. Mix in the spinach purée and tomatoes. Cover tightly and cook on a low heat for about 35 minutes or until the chicken is tender.
6. Remove the lid and if there is any liquid remaining then continue cooking and stirring until all the liquid evaporates and the oil separates out.
7. Just before serving, pour the cream over the chicken and serve immediately.

Serve hot with nans or any Indian bread.

Suitable for freezing without the cream.

Punjab Egg Curry
(Ande di Curry)
SERVES 4

A *classic example of the heights to which eggs can be raised! Hard-boiled eggs are simmered in a rich gravy to make a dish that is a treat for all egg lovers.*

200g (7 oz) onions
125ml (4 fl oz) corn oil
30g (1 oz) fresh root ginger, peeled and grated
2 whole cloves
2 bay leaves
2 green cardamoms
1 teaspoon ground turmeric
1 teaspoon ground dried red chillies
1 teaspoon ground coriander seeds
salt, to taste
100g (3$^1/_2$ oz) fresh tomatoes, chopped
1 tablespoon white poppy seeds
500ml (16 fl oz) water
6 hard-boiled eggs, shelled
60ml (2 fl oz) thick double cream
$^1/_2$ teaspoon Indian garam masala

Preparation time: 20 minutes
Cooking time: 35 minutes

1. Slice 90g (3 oz) of the onions and grate the remaining 125g (4 oz).
2. Put the oil in a deep heavy-based saucepan and fry the sliced onions until they are crisp and dark brown. Remove, crush and set aside.
3. In the same oil, fry the grated onions on a high heat until light golden. Add the ginger and fry for 2-3 minutes.
4. Add the cloves, bay leaves and cardamoms and fry for a few seconds. Lower the heat and stir in the turmeric, ground red chillies and coriander. After about 30 seconds, add the salt and the tomatoes. Increase the heat and keep frying until the tomatoes are well blended.
5. Grind the poppy seeds and add about 4 table-spoons of water to make a fine paste. Add this to the hot mixture, and after 1 minute, stir in the water, mixing it in well. Bring to the boil, cover and reduce the heat. Simmer for 5-6 minutes until a fairly thick gravy is formed. Add the crushed, fried onions and mix well.
6. Halve the eggs and lower them gently into the gravy. Carefully stir in the cream. Cover and cook on a very low heat for a further 4-5 minutes. Remove from the heat and leave undisturbed for a few minutes before serving sprinkled with the garam masala.

Serve with rice.

Unsuitable for freezing.

FISH DISHES

Balti Fish Curry
SERVES 2-3

*I*n Baltistan they use dried fish for this recipe and serve it with rice. The ajowan *(carom seeds) and garlic are added to kill the strong fish flavour and the yogurt gives a sour taste which goes very well with the fish.*

500g (1 lb) coley or cod, cut
    into 10cm (4 inch) pieces
2 tablespoons cooking oil
1 teaspoon ground fresh root
    ginger
1 tablespoon ground fresh
    garlic
$^1/_2$ teaspoon ground turmeric
$^1/_2$ teaspoon salt
$^1/_2$ teaspoon red chilli powder
$^1/_2$ teaspoon ajowan
1 tablespoon ground coriander
3 tablespoons natural low fat
    yogurt
2 tablespoons chopped fresh
    coriander
1 teaspoon Balti garam masala

Preparation time: 10 minutes
Cooking time: 30 minutes

1. Wash the fish pieces in cold water and drain in a colander for 15 minutes.
2. Put the oil in a karahi or deep frying pan, add the ginger and garlic and stir-fry for 1-2 minutes or until they change colour. Add the turmeric, salt, red chilli powder, ajowan and ground coriander and mix well. Cook, uncovered, on a low heat for 5 minutes.
3. Add the yogurt and stir well. The mixture will be a bit runny so keep it uncovered and cook on a low heat, stirring from time to time, until oil separates out and excess liquid evaporates – the bhun method. If the mixture starts sticking stir in 2 tablespoons of water.
4. Gently lower the fish pieces into the karahi and cook, uncovered, on medium heat for 7-10 minutes or until cooked. Put the karahi on the table, garnish with fresh coriander and garam masala.
5. To serve with rice, add 150-300ml ($^1/_4$-$^1/_2$ pint) of boiling water to the finished dish. Simmer, covered, for 5 minutes. Remove from the heat and keep dish covered for 5 minutes, for oil to rise to the top, before serving.

Serve with nans or chapattis.

Suitable for freezing – if fresh fish is used.

Previous pages: Balti Dry Fish (p.57) and Balti fish Curry

Balti Dry Fish
SERVES 2

*T*his *is an interesting recipe in which gram (chick-pea) flour is used dry. The fish is fried with a touch of oil on a very large griddle or tawa. It is crisp and tender and eaten hot off the griddle with chapattis or on its own with a yogurt raita and chutneys. Gram flour is readily available in most supermarkets and Asian grocers.*

500g (1 lb) whole trout, cleaned and gutted or coley or cod, cut into 10cm (4 inch) pieces
1 teaspoon salt
1 tablespoon ground fresh garlic
1 tablespoon ground fresh root ginger
1 teaspoon ground fresh green chillies
90g (3 oz) gram (chick-pea) flour
1 teaspoon red chilli powder
1 teaspoon ground turmeric
1 tablespoon ground coriander
1 teaspoon ground cumin
1 teaspoon ajowan
2 tablespoons Balti garam masala
4 tablespoons finely chopped fresh coriander
4 tablespoons oil

Preparation time: 15 minutes, plus 1-2 hours marinating
Cooking time: 20 minutes

1. Wash the fish in cold water and drain in a colander for 5 minutes. Make a paste using half the salt and all the garlic, ginger and green chillies. Apply to the fish and leave in a cool place to marinate for 1-2 hours.
2. Put the gram flour on a large flat plate. Add the remaining salt, all the red chilli powder, turmeric, ground coriander, ground cumin, ajowan, half the garam masala and half the fresh coriander. Mix well using your hands, so the gram flour is well seasoned.
3. Add 2 tablespoons of oil to a griddle/tawa or a non-stick frying pan and switch on the heat. Take one piece of marinated fish, dip into the dry flour until well coated all over. Coat all the pieces of fish and put on a large flat plate.
4. Gently lower pieces of fish into the hot oil. Fry 2-3 pieces of fish at a time depending on the size of the pan used. Cook, uncovered, on a low heat for 5-10 minutes each side or until fish is well browned. Add more oil as necessary.
5. Remove fish and put into a serving dish and garnish with the remaining garam masala and fresh coriander before serving.

Serve with nans or chapattis with yogurt and chutney.

Unsuitable for freezing.

Balti Battered Fish

SERVES 3-4

In Baltistan, they have their own version of fish and chips. They make some chapattis before the fish is fried, then everyone takes a chapatti in their hand, and the cooked fish is placed directly on to the chapatti. Yogurt and mint chutney is spooned on top and as no plates are used, there is no washing up!

$1\frac{1}{2}$ teaspoons salt

700g ($1\frac{1}{2}$ lb) coley or cod fillets, approx 10-15cm (4-6 inch) long and 1-2.5 cm ($\frac{1}{2}$-1 inch) thick

125g (4 oz) gram (chick-pea) flour

1 teaspoon ajowan

1 teaspoon red chilli powder

3 tablespoons natural yogurt

1 teaspoon ground fresh garlic

distilled white or malt vinegar to make batter

oil for deep frying

4 tablespoons plain or wholemeal flour

Preparation time: 15 minutes
Cooking time: 30-40 minutes

1. Sprinkle 1 teaspoon of the salt over the unwashed fish and leave in a cool place for 2-4 hours.

2. Wash the fish thoroughly and drain well in a colander.

3. Put the gram flour, ajowan, red chilli powder, remaining salt, yogurt and garlic into a deep bowl. Add enough vinegar to make a thick, smooth batter.

4. Half fill a karahi or deep pan with oil and heat on medium heat. Check the temperature of the oil by dropping in a small piece of bread. It should turn golden brown in 1 minute.

5. Dip individual pieces of fish into the plain or wholemeal flour (this will help the batter to stay on), then dip into the batter.

6. Lower gently into the oil and deep fry 2 or 3 pieces at a time for 7-10 minutes on each side, or until the fish is golden brown.

7. Remove, drain on kitchen paper and finish frying the remaining fish in the same way.

Serve with nans or chapattis with yogurt, mint chutney and fresh salad. Alternatively serve with chips and vegetables.

Unsuitable for freezing.

Balti Battered Fish

Upper Lake Kachura Fish
SERVES 5-6

This dish is like a broth and is very nourishing. The original recipe used sun-dried powdered tomatoes and sun-dried onions ground in a pestle and mortar but here tomato purée and fresh onions are used instead.

1.15 litres (2 pints) water
1 teaspoon salt
1 teaspoon Balti garam masala
125g (4 oz) carrots, diced
125g (4 oz) fresh or frozen peas
125g (4 oz) onions, diced
125g (4 oz) frozen or canned
    sweetcorn
90g (3 oz) potatoes, diced
4 tablespoons tomato purée
500g (1 lb) haddock, coley or
    cod, cut into 2.5 cm (1 inch)
    pieces
4 tablespoons porridge oats

Preparation time: 15 minutes
Cooking time: 30 minutes

1. Put the water, salt and garam masala into a saucepan, bring to the boil then add the carrots, peas and onions. Simmer, covered, for 7 minutes then add the sweetcorn and potatoes and simmer for 20-30 minutes until all the vegetables are soft and the mixture thickens.
2. Add the tomato purée and stir well. Add the fish pieces and porridge oats and simmer, uncovered, for 7-10 minutes or until the fish and oats are cooked. Don't stir too often or vigorously as the fish will disintegrate.

Serve in a small individual bowls to be sipped without using spoons.

Unsuitable for freezing.

Satpara Lake Fish

SERVES 1-2

Satpara Lake is a few kilometres from Skardu, the capital of Baltistan. Fresh fish can be caught in nearby trout farms and cooked as described below.

1 small whole trout, approx
   500g (1 lb) in weight
1 teaspoon salt
$\frac{1}{2}$ teaspoon red chilli powder
1 tablespoon Balti garam
   masala
1 tablespoon oil
2 tablespoons lemon juice

Preparation time: 5 minutes, plus 30 minutes marinating
Cooking time: 20 minutes

1. Clean the fish inside out, remove the gut and the scales. Wash the fish and drain in a colander for 15 minutes. Make long slits on both sides of the fish.
2. Mix together the salt, red chilli powder, garam masala, oil and the lemon juice in a bowl.
3. Spread the mixture all over the fish, taking care to push well into the slits. Leave in a cool place to marinate for 30 minutes.
4. Place a layer of foil on the grill rack, put fish on the foil and place under a preheated grill. Cook on each side for 7-10 minutes or until fish is tender. Alternatively deep fry in oil to a crisp golden brown.

Serve with mashed potato, salad or chips and any chutney.

Unsuitable for freezing.

Fish Dishes

Dhum Fish
SERVES 2-3

The Baltis cook this in an oven in the ground, surrounding the fish with a clay paste. You can achieve similar results using the grill. The ajowan is only used to kill off the strong flavour of the fish and may be omitted if it is difficult to obtain.

500g (1 lb) coley or cod fillets
1 teaspoon coriander seeds
1 teaspoon white cumin seeds
3 tablespoons lemon juice
1 teaspoon ajowan
1/2 teaspoon coarsely ground
   dried red chillies
1/2 teaspoon salt
1 tablespoons ground fresh
   garlic
1/2 teaspoon ground turmeric

Preparation time: 10 minutes, plus 2-4 hours marinating
Cooking time: 30 minutes

1. Wash the fish with cold water and drain in a colander for 15 minutes.
2. Heat a non-stick frying pan until hot, add the coriander and cumin seeds and dry roast for 30-40 seconds or until the mixture gives off an aroma. Cool and grind in a coffee grinder.
3. Put the lemon juice in a bowl, add the ground cumin and coriander, ajowan, red chillies, salt, garlic, and turmeric and mix together to form a thick paste. Spread the paste over both sides of each fish fillet. Cover and leave in a cool place for 2-4 hours.
4. Arrange the fillets on a grill rack. Cook under a preheated grill for 10 minutes each side or until fish is tender. Use a fish slice and be gentle when turning over on to the second side, as the fish may fall apart. Alternatively, deep fry the fish, 2 or 3 pieces at a time, in vegetable oil.

Serve with a salad, chapattis and chutney.

Suitable for freezing: after Stage 4, place the fish pieces 5cm (2 inch) apart on a large tray and freeze for 3 hours. Remove pieces and freeze in bags. Deep fry from frozen.

Dhum Fish

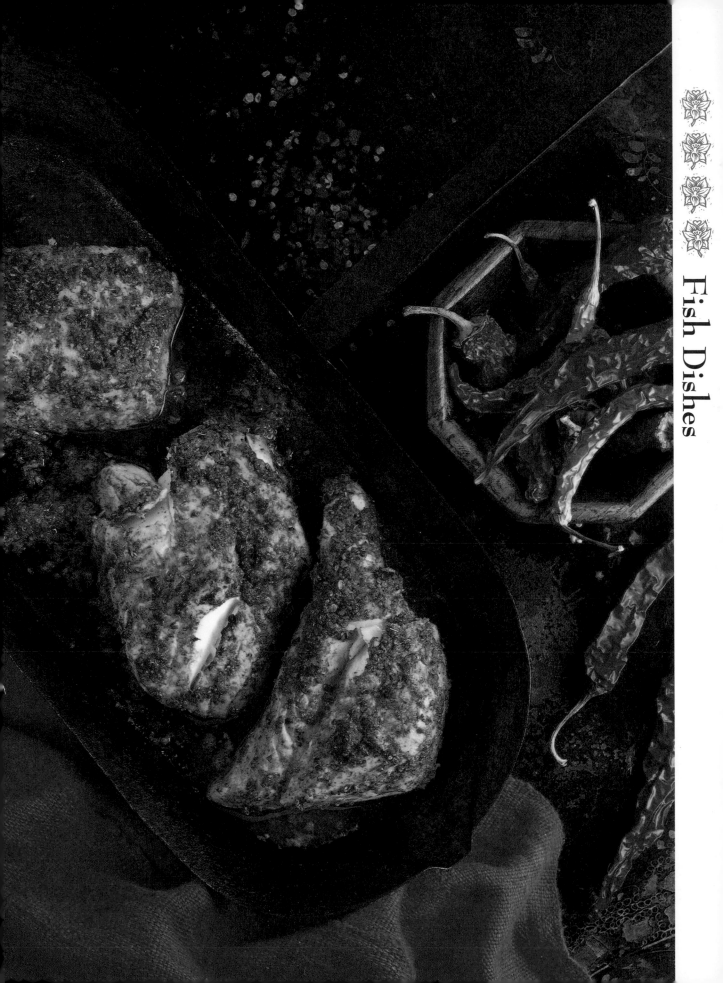

Fish Pilao
SERVES 4-6

Trout is often used in this dish, but you can use any firm white fish instead. In Baltistan powdered sun-dried tomatoes would be used and for this tomato purée has been substituted.

500g (1 lb) of skinned and
    filleted trout, coley or cod,
    cut into 5cm (2 inch) pieces
4 tablespoons oil or ghee
125g (4 oz) finely sliced onions
1½ teaspoons salt
1 teaspoon red chilli powder
1 teaspoon ground turmeric
10cm (4 inch) piece cassia
4 whole cloves
6 black peppercorns
1 teaspoon whole cumin seeds
1 teaspoon coriander seeds
4 tablespoons tomato purée
1 tablespoon ground fresh
    garlic
850ml (1½ pints) water
500g (1 lb) basmati rice,
    soaked in water for
    30 minutes

Preparation time: 10 minutes
Cooking time: 30 minutes

1. Wash the fish in cold water and drain well in a colander.
2. Heat the oil in a large pan and fry the onions until brown. Use a slotted spoon to remove the fried onions onto a plate and leave the oil in the pan.
3. To this oil, add the salt, red chilli powder, turmeric, cassia, cloves, peppercorns, cumin and coriander. Stir-fry for 2 minutes. Add the tomato purée and garlic and mix well. Add the water and bring to the boil.
4. Gently lower the fish into the spice mixture but do not stir as the fish will break up. Add the browned onions and simmer, uncovered, for 5 minutes or until fish is cooked. Remove the fish very gently using a slotted spoon, and put on a large flat plate.
5. Add the rice to the mixture in the pan and bring to the boil. Cook, covered, on medium heat for 7 minutes or until the mixture is nearly dry. Turn heat to lowest setting.
6. Pile the fish on top of the rice. Put a layer of foil on top of the pan, place lid on top to seal tightly and cook for about 15 minutes or until rice is cooked. (Or put in preheated oven 180˚C, 350˚F, Gas Mark 4 for 15 minutes.)

Serve with any raita or natural yogurt.

Unsuitable for freezing.

Fish and Potato Kebabs
SERVES 4-5

These kebabs can be eaten on their own or with a curry gravy. This recipe uses coley, but canned tuna in brine can be used instead.

250g (8 oz) potatoes
250g (8oz) coley or 200g (7 oz) canned tuna in brine, drained
2 tablespoons chopped fresh coriander
1/2 teaspoon finely chopped green chillies
1/2 teaspoon salt, or to taste
1 teaspoon Balti garam masala
60g (2 oz) finely chopped spring onions
1 egg
oil for deep frying

Preparation time: 15 minutes
Cooking time: 10 minutes

1. Boil the potatoes, drain, peel and mash. Set aside to cool. If using coley, wash in cold water and then steam or cook in a microwave. Cool completely and flake.
2. Put the coley or flaked tuna, into a deep bowl. Add the potatoes, coriander, chillies, salt, garam masala and spring onions and mix well.
3. Beat the egg in a small bowl. Add enough egg to the fish mixture to bind. Divide the mixture into 8-10 equal pieces. Take each piece, make into a round and then shape into an oval. Put all the kebabs on a flat plate keeping them apart.
4. Put the oil in a karahi or deep pan and heat on a medium heat. Check the temperature by dropping in a tiny piece of mixture, if it rises to the top immediately, the oil is ready for frying the kebabs. Fry 3 or 4 kebabs in the oil for 5-7 minutes or until browned. Remove with a slotted spoon and drain on kitchen paper.

Serve on a flat plate, garnished with lettuce, cucumber, tomato and lemon and accompany with ketchup or any chutney.

Suitable for freezing.

Fish Dishes

Baked Fish
(Tandoori Machi)
SERVES 4

This is a dish that needs very little effort, but which produces mouth-watering results. The special 'roasted' flavour which a 'tandoor' gives makes this into an exciting delicacy, but it can be done almost as well in a conventional oven.

4 fresh, cleaned and gutted trout, each weighing about 300g (10 oz)

15g (½ oz) fresh root ginger, peeled

3 cloves of garlic, peeled

2 tablespoons natural yogurt

1 tablespoon lemon juice

1 teaspoon white wine vinegar

1 tablespoon mustard oil

1 teaspoon dried fenugreek leaves

½ teaspoon dried mint

½ teaspoon cumin seeds

½ teaspoon ground dried red chillies

¼ teaspoon Indian garam masala

salt, to taste

4 drops natural orange food colour, optional

1 tablespoon fresh coriander leaves

Preparation time: 20 minutes, plus marinating
Cooking time: 15 minutes

1. Make 2 long incisions across both sides of each fish and put in a shallow dish.
2. Put the ginger, garlic, yogurt, lemon juice, vinegar, oil, fenugreek leaves, mint, cumin seeds, ground red chillies, garam masala, salt, colouring (if used) and coriander leaves into a liquidiser and process until well blended.
3. Pour the mixture over the fish, coating them thoroughly all over. Cover and leave in a cool place for 2-3 hours.
4. Preheat the oven to 200°C, 400°F, Gas Mark 6. Place the marinated fish on a rack in a baking tin and bake for 15 minutes. Turn the fish over once after about 10 minutes to cook the fish on both sides.
5. Just before serving, put the tray under a preheated grill and brown the fish on both sides for 1-2 minutes, to give a barbecued look.

Serve with chutney and onion relish.

Unsuitable for freezing.

Baked Fish and Carom Flavoured Fish (p.68)

Carom Flavoured Fish
(Machi Amritsari)
SERVES 4

*P*unjabi cuisine has a limited range of fish dishes. The few that are made are usually fried and tend to be served as a snack, rather than as a main meal. The men of 'the land of five rivers' are known to be fond of 'a peg or two' and what better than a drink and some fried fish to finish off a hard days work!

750g (1½ lb) firm, white, fillet of fish, (eg. cod), cut into 7.5 x 5cm (3 x 2 inch) pieces
2 tablespoons lemon juice
salt
125g (4 oz) gram (chick-pea) flour
45g (1½ oz) fresh root ginger, peeled and finely chopped
4 cloves of garlic, peeled and finely chopped
1 teaspoon Indian garam masala
½ teaspoon ground turmeric
1 teaspoon ground dried red chillies
½ teaspoon ground black pepper
½-1 teaspoon carom seeds
1 teaspoon lemon juice
about 250ml (8 fl oz) water
oil for deep frying

Preparation time: 30 minutes
Cooking time: 15 minutes

1. Place the fish in a bowl and add the lemon juice and 1 teaspoon salt and mix well. Leave to marinate for 10 minutes. Drain off all the liquid and dry the pieces well with absorbent paper.
2. Sieve the gram flour into a bowl and add the ginger, garlic, garam masala, turmeric, ground red chillies, pepper, carom seeds, salt to taste and lemon juice. Add the water a little at a time to make a batter of coating consistency. Use more or less of the water as required.
3. Heat the oil in a kadhai or deep heavy-based frying pan. When the oil is hot, reduce the heat. Dip the pieces of fish in the batter and fry 2 or 3 pieces at a time. Be careful not to brown the pieces too quickly. Keeping the heat on medium to low, fry the fish until they are golden brown, crisp all over and fully cooked.
Remove from the oil and drain on absorbent paper.

Serve with any chutney and fresh salad.

Unsuitable for freezing.

Fried Fish
(Tali Machi)
SERVES 4

Fried fish invariably means fish fried in batter in the West, but in India, most people use no batter at all. This style of Punjabi 'tali machi' is perhaps one of the easiest and most common methods of making a simple dish which looks as good as it tastes.

750g (1½ lb) firm, white fish fillet, cut into 5cm (2 inch) cubes
2 tablespoons white wine or cider vinegar
salt
1 teaspoon turmeric
2 fresh green chillies, finely chopped
2 tablespoons ground coriander seeds, crushed or ground
1 tablespoon fresh mint leaves, finely chopped
1 teaspoon ground dried red chillies
1 tablespoon Indian garam masala
2 tablespoons lemon juice
oil for deep frying

Preparation time: 15 minutes
Cooking time: 10 minutes

1. Place the fish in a bowl and add the vinegar, ½ teaspoon salt and the turmeric and mix well. Leave to marinate for 10 minutes. Drain off all the liquid and dry the pieces well on absorbent paper.
2. Add the chillies, coriander, mint, ground red chillies, garam masala and salt to taste, to the fish and mix well.
3. Add the lemon juice (add a little more if desired) and let the seasoned fish stand for about 5 minutes.
4. Heat the oil in a kadhai or deep heavy-based frying pan on a medium heat. When the oil is quite hot, reduce the heat and fry two or three pieces of fish at a time until well cooked and golden brown. Drain the fish on absorbent paper.

Serve with any chutney or tomato ketchup, which is as popular in India as it is in the West.

Unsuitable for freezing.

Fish Dishes

VEGETABLE DISHES AND DHALS

Balti Okra Masala
(Masala Bindi)
SERVES 2

*O*kra is always fried before cooking or adding to meat as it gives off a sticky gluey substance. There is an art to cooking okra, because if they are cut very small they will simply disintegrate when stirred. Do not cut them any smaller than stated in this recipe.

500g (1 lb) okra
4 tablespoons oil
250g (8 oz) onion, cut into thin
   slices
1 tablespoon grated fresh root
   ginger
125g (4 oz) finely chopped
   fresh tomatoes
1 teaspoon salt
$^1/_2$ teaspoon ground turmeric
1 teaspoon ground fresh green
   chillies (reduce for mild taste)
2 tablespoons whole coriander
   leaves

Preparation time: 15 minutes
Cooking time: 15 minutes

1. When buying okra, always pick the small firm ones as they are easier to cook. Wash the okra in cold water and wipe off excess water with kitchen paper. Cut off tops and tails of okra and either leave okra whole or cut into 5cm (2 inch) pieces.
2. Put the oil into a karahi or deep frying pan, add the onions and fry until they are transparent. Add the ginger, tomatoes, salt, turmeric and chillies. Simmer mixture on low heat for 7-10 minutes or until the liquid is reduced.
3. Add the okra and stir once. Simmer for 10 minutes on low heat or until okra is cooked but still firm to touch. Do not stir too often as okra is a very delicate vegetable and may break up. Sprinkle with coriander leaves.

Serve with a raita and chapattis.

Unsuitable for freezing.

Previous pages: Balti Okra Masala, Balti Potatoes and Coriander (p.73) and Balti Masoor Dhal (p.81)

Balti Potatoes and Coriander
(Aloo Dhaniya)
SERVES 3-4

*I*n India they make a very similar dish with potatoes and fenugreek leaves. However, in Baltistan they love coriander and since it is scarce and not readily available throughout the year, when they do find it they add it to almost everything.

250g (8 oz) fresh coriander

2 tablespoons oil

125g (4 oz) grated or finely chopped onion

1 teaspoon ground fresh garlic

250g (8 oz) peeled potato, cut into 2.5cm (1 inch) cubes

1 teaspoon salt

$^1/_2$ teaspoon red chilli powder (omit for a milder taste)

$^1/_2$ teaspoon ground turmeric

1 teaspoon ground fresh green chillies (optional)

1 tablespoons ghee or 2 tablespoons oil

1 teaspoon grated fresh root ginger

Preparation time: 20 minutes

Cooking time: 40 minutes

1. To prepare the coriander, take off the leaves from the stalks, add to a large bowl with plenty of water and soak for 20 seconds for the silt to settle to the bottom. Gently remove the leaves and chop finely or blend in a food processor.

2. Put the oil in a karahi or deep frying pan, add the onions and fry until transparent. Add the garlic and fry for 1 minute then add the potatoes, salt, red chilli powder and turmeric. Cook on lowest heat setting for 5 minutes or until potatoes are par-cooked.

3. Add the coriander and fresh chillies if used and mix once. Simmer on low heat, for 10 minutes or until potatoes are fully cooked. Stir from time to time to prevent mixture from sticking to the bottom. If the potatoes are cooked but liquid remains, cook uncovered until it evaporates.

4. In a small frying pan add the ghee and grated ginger and cook on low heat for 1 minute until brown. Pour on top of the vegetables in the karahi – this is called tarka. Take to the table to serve, without mixing.

Serve with warm nans or chapattis brushed with some oil or butter and a bowl of natural yogurt and thin slices of mooli (white radish).

Unsuitable for freezing.

Balti Dhal and Marrow
(Dhal Kadu)
SERVES 3-4

*K*adu is a type of marrow; a very pale green, hard-skinned vegetable with a pith of white pulp and small seeds. The skin is discarded. It can be long and thin or round with a stalk at the end. Once cooked, it softens into a lovely textured vegetable similar to courgettes and turnips but with a different aroma. Kadu is available at Asian grocery stores. Use turnips or courgettes if not available.

180g (6 oz) split skinless lentils (Masoor dhal)

600ml (1 pint) water

1 teaspoon salt

$1/2$ teaspoon red chilli powder

$1/2$ teaspoon ground turmeric

2 tablespoons oil

60g (2 oz) grated onion

2 tablespoons tomato purée

250g (8 oz) kadu (Indian pumpkin), peeled and cut into 1cm ($1/2$ inch) dice

1 tablespoons ghee or 2 table spoons oil

2 cloves garlic, finely sliced

1 teaspoon Balti garam masala

1 tablespoon chopped fresh coriander

Preparation time: 15 minutes
Cooking time: 35 minutes

1. Wash the dhal in 2 or 3 changes of water and soak in warm water for 20 minutes. Strain and discard the water.

2. Put the dhal in a large pan, add the measured water, salt, red chilli powder and turmeric. Bring to the boil, then simmer, covered, for 15 minutes or until the dhal is cooked. Either whisk carefully using a hand whisk, or mix well with a spoon to form a mixture resembling a broth. Remove from the heat and put aside.

3. Heat the oil in a pan and add the onion and sauté until golden. Add the tomato purée and kadu and simmer for 10 minutes on low heat or until kadu is cooked. Add a tablespoon of water at a time if required, to achieve this stage.

4. Add the cooke[1] kadu to the dhal. Return to the heat and simmer together for 5 minutes. Transfer into a serving dish or a steel karahi.

5. In a small frying pan add the ghee or oil and garlic slices. When the garlic begins to change colour, pour onto the dhal and kadu. Garnish with garam masala and fresh coriander.

Serve with plain rice or any bread.

Suitable for freezing.

Balti Potatoes and Cauliflower (p.76) and Balti Dhal and Marrow

Balti Potatoes and Cauliflower
(*Aloo Gobi*)
SERVES 3-4

*T*he cauliflowers that are on sale in Baltistan are often rather limp because they have to be transported on a long journey through the cold. Aloo Gobi, however, is very tasty as the 'tarka' added at the end livens up the cauliflower.

3 tablespoons oil

60g (2 oz) grated or finely chopped onion

1 tablespoons ground fresh root ginger

250g (8 oz) finely chopped tomatoes or 200g (7 oz) can chopped tomatoes

1 teaspoon salt

$\frac{1}{2}$ teaspoon ground turmeric

$\frac{1}{4}$ teaspoon red chilli powder

250g (8 oz) potatoes, peeled and diced into 2.5cm (1 inch) cubes

250g (8 oz) cauliflower, cut into 2.5cm (1 inch) florets

1 tablespoon ghee

2 tablespoons grated fresh root ginger

1 teaspoon whole cumin seeds

1 tablespoons chopped fresh coriander

1 teaspoon Balti garam masala

Preparation time: 5 minutes
Cooking time: 25 minutes

1. Put the oil and the onion in a karahi or deep frying pan and cook on medium heat until the onions turn transparent. Add the ground ginger and fry for 30 seconds, then add the tomatoes, salt, turmeric and red chilli powder. Simmer on low heat for 10 minutes or until the onions and tomatoes form a pulp, the oil separates out and the excess liquid evaporates.

2. Add the potatoes and 2 tablespoons of water. Cook, covered, on the lowest heat setting for 5 minutes or until potatoes are par-cooked. Add 2 tablespoons of water if required. Add cauliflower florets and 2 tablespoons water. Cook, covered, on a low heat setting for 15 minutes or until vegetables are cooked. Remove from heat.

3. In a small frying pan add the ghee and grated ginger and cook on low heat for 1-2 minutes until brown. Add the cumin seeds and pour the whole mixture (the tarka) into the karahi, over the vegetables. Sprinkle with coriander and garam masala.

Serve with hot chapattis, spread with ghee or butter.

Unsuitable for freezing.

Balti Okra Fry
(Talli Bindi)
SERVES 2-3

The okra is left whole in this recipe which is very quick and easy to make as it uses a stir-fry method. When selecting Okra, avoid using those that are large or limp and choose small firm ones.

500g (1 lb) okra
4 tablespoons corn oil
$\frac{1}{2}$ teaspoon salt
$\frac{1}{2}$ teaspoon red chilli powder
$\frac{1}{4}$ teaspoon ground turmeric
$\frac{1}{2}$ teaspoon ground coriander
125g (4 oz) chopped fresh tomatoes
250g (8 oz) finely sliced onion
2 tablespoons chopped fresh coriander
1 finely sliced fresh green chilli (optional)
1 teaspoon Balti garam masala

Preparation time: 15 minutes
Cooking time: 20 minutes

1. Rinse the okra under cold water in a colander, wipe dry with kitchen towel. Carefully chop off the tops and a little of the tails. Put in a bowl.
2. Add the oil to a karahi or wok and when slightly hot, add the okra, then the salt, red chilli powder, turmeric and ground coriander. Stir ONCE, keep on medium heat, uncovered, for 5 minutes, then add the tomatoes. Turn the okra over gently with a flat wooden spoon. Cook, covered, for a further 10 minutes or until okra is cooked.
3. Add the onions, fresh coriander, fresh green chilli and garam masala and toss gently. Leave on high heat, uncovered, for 2 minutes. The onions should remain crunchy.

Serve with natural yogurt and chapattis, nans or puris.

Unsuitable for freezing.

Vegetable Dishes and Dhals

Balti Chick-peas
(Chanay Ka Shorba)
SERVES 3-4

*C*hick-peas or channas are cheap, filling and nourishing. They come in two varieties, the large light-skinned ones and the tiny dark-skinned ones. The following recipe is rather like a soup. A chapatti or nan is broken into small bite-size pieces and put in a bowl, the chick-pea curry is ladled on top and after 5 minutes the bread pieces have absorbed the curry and 'swollen'.

125ml (4 fl oz) oil
125g (4 oz) grated onion
$^1/_2$ teaspoon ground fresh root
   ginger
$^1/_2$ teaspoon ground fresh garlic
125g (4 oz) finely chopped
   fresh tomatoes
350g (12 oz) cooked or canned
   chick-peas, drained
$^1/_2$ teaspoon salt
$^1/_2$ teaspoon red chilli powder
a pinch of ground turmeric
600ml (1 pint) water
1 whole fresh green chilli
2 tablespoons chopped fresh
   coriander
1 teaspoon Balti garam masala

Preparation time: 10 minutes
Cooking time: 20 minutes

1. Put the oil into a karahi or deep frying pan, add the onions and fry for 5 minutes or until golden brown. Add the ginger, garlic and tomatoes and simmer, covered, for 10-15 minutes on low heat until the oil separates and the mixture forms a pulp. Add a tablespoon of water at a time if required.
2. Add the cooked or canned chick-peas, salt, red chilli powder and turmeric and stir well. Add 6 tablespoons of boiling water and simmer on low heat for 5-7 minutes or until excess liquid evaporates and there is a thick gravy. The dish can be served at this stage as a masala curry.
3. For a 'runny' curry, add 300-425ml ($^1/_2$-$^3/_4$ pint) of boiling water and simmer again on low heat for 10-15 minutes. Increase or decrease amount of water to your liking.
4. Add the whole chilli, coriander and garam masala. Remove from the heat and leave, covered, for 5 minutes or until the oil rises to the top.

Serve with rice and plain salad.

Suitable for freezing.

Balti Chick-peas and Balti Aubergine Bhartha (p.80)

Balti Aubergine Bhartha
(Bengun Bartha)
SERVES 4-5

*A*lthough this dish is made in many parts of India and Pakistan, in Baltistan it has a slightly different touch, in that the aubergines are roasted on the embers created by the wooden fire used for other cooking. The bhartha has a strong chargrilled taste and flavour.

500g (1 lb) aubergines

3 tablespoons corn oil

1 teaspoon whole cumin seeds

1 teaspoon ground fresh garlic

125g (4 oz) chopped fresh
  tomatoes

½ teaspoon salt

½ teaspoon red chilli powder
  (omit for a milder taste)

¼ teaspoon ground turmeric

1 teaspoon ground coriander

1 teaspoon ground cumin

90g (3 oz) onions finely sliced
  lengthways or spring onions,
  finely chopped

1 teaspoon chopped fresh green
  chillies

6 tablespoons chopped fresh
  coriander

1 teaspoon Balti garam masala

Preparation time: 15 minutes
Cooking time: 20 minutes

1. If aubergines are fist-sized or smaller, bake them whole under a preheated grill for 4 minutes each side or until brown on all sides. If the aubergine is large (e.g. Dutch) then cut in half and grill both sides. Lower gently into cold water to cool, then carefully peel off the skin and discard. Chop up or use a fork to mash the aubergine into a coarse pulp.

2. Put the oil into a small karahi or large frying pan, add the whole cumin and garlic and when the mixture sizzles, add the aubergine pulp, tomatoes, salt, red chilli powder and turmeric. Stir well, then simmer, covered, on low heat for 10 minutes. If the mixture begins to stick to the bottom add 2 tablespoons of water and stir.

3. Add the coriander and cumin and simmer, covered, for 2 minutes. Finally add the onions, fresh chillies, fresh coriander and garam masala. Remove from the heat and keep, covered, for 5 minutes before serving.

Serve with chapattis or plain rice.

Suitable for freezing.

Balti Masoor Dhal

SERVES 4-5

A variety of pulses and lentils are eaten in the region and the quickest one to prepare is masoor dhal (red lentils). It goes a long way so it is made quite often as a cheap alternative to meat as a source of protein.

250g (8 oz) split skinless lentils (masoor dhal)

600ml (1 pint) water, approx

1 teaspoon salt

$\frac{1}{2}$ teaspoon red chilli powder

$\frac{1}{4}$ teaspoon ground turmeric

4 cloves of garlic, peeled and 2 small cloves of garlic, peeled and thinly sliced

60g (2 oz) chopped fresh tomatoes

2 tablespoons ghee or 4 table spoons corn oil

1 sliced fresh green chilli (optional)

2 tablespoons chopped fresh coriander

1 teaspoon Balti garam masala

Preparation time: 10 minutes plus soaking time
Cooking time: 15 minutes

1. Wash the dhal in 2 or 3 changes of water and soak in warm water for 30 minutes. Drain and discard the water.
2. Put the dhal into a karahi or saucepan and add just enough water to cover the dhal. Add the salt, chilli powder, turmeric, whole garlic cloves and tomatoes. Bring to the boil then simmer, covered, for 10 minutes or until dhal is cooked but still whole.
3. In a small frying pan heat the ghee or oil and add the garlic slices. Once they start to sizzle and turn slightly brown, remove from the heat. Pour onto the dhal in the karahi but do not stir.
4. Garnish with fresh chilli slices, if liked, coriander and garam masala. Do not stir. The beauty of this dish is to serve with a top layer of fat, and if you use ghee it will have a silky look and texture.

Serve with chapattis, nans or rice. If serving with rice, increase the amount of water so the dhal is more liquid.

Suitable for freezing.

Balti Dhal with Potatoes
(Dhal Aloo)
SERVES 4

*I*n the rest of the country dhal is either cooked on its own or with meat, but in
Baltistan it is cooked with potatoes too. *This thick creamy dish is often served with
rice mixed with peas and a small lump of pure ghee.*

125g (4 oz) split skinless
  moong dhal
2 tablespoons oil
1 teaspoon grated fresh root
  ginger
1 teaspoon ground fresh garlic
125g (4 oz) finely chopped
  fresh tomatoes or 2 tablespoons tomato purée
600ml (1 pint) water
1 teaspoon salt
$\frac{1}{2}$ teaspoon red chilli powder
$\frac{1}{2}$ teaspoon ground turmeric
500g (1 lb) potatoes, peeled
  and cut into 2.5cm (1 inch)
  cubes
1 tablespoons chopped fresh
  coriander
1 teaspoon Balti garam masala

Preparation time: 10 minutes plus soaking time
Cooking time: 45 minutes

1. Wash the dhal in 2 or 3 changes of water and
soak in warm water for 4 hours or overnight.
Drain the dhal and discard the water.
2. Put the oil in a karahi or saucepan, add the ginger and garlic and fry on high heat for 30 seconds.
Add the tomatoes and stir once. Turn the heat to
medium and add the dhal, water, salt, red chilli
powder and turmeric. Bring to the boil and simmer, covered, on low heat for 30 minutes or until
dhal is cooked.
3. Carefully blend the dhal well with the liquid
using a flat wooden spoon, or a hand or electric
blender. This will result in a creamy broth. Add
more water if the mixture is too thick and boil,
uncovered, if it is too runny.
4. Add the potatoes, simmer on low heat for
10 minutes or until potatoes are cooked. The
result should be a creamy broth with potatoes. If it
is too thin, boil, uncovered, until the liquid is
reduced. If it is too dry, add a little water and simmer for 5 minutes. Sprinkle with the coriander and
garam masala.

Serve with plain boiled rice or nans.

Unsuitable for freezing.

Balti Dhal with Spinach (p.84) and Balti Dhal with Potatoes

Vegetable Dishes and Dhals

Balti Dhal with Spinach
(Dhal Palak)
SERVES 3-4

Strangely enough this dish uses yogurt in the cooking process. Milk is very expensive in Baltistan and they use a lot of dried milk powder made up, as and when required. Yogurt is made out of this milk and due to the full fat content of the milk powder, it makes a firm, creamy yogurt.

60g (2 oz) split skinless channa dhal

500g (1 lb) fresh spinach or 250g (8 oz) canned or frozen spinach

600ml (1 pint) water

4 tablespoons natural yogurt

1 teaspoon salt

½ teaspoon red chilli powder

½ teaspoon ground turmeric

1 teaspoon ground fresh garlic

1 teaspoon ground fresh root ginger

3 tablespoons oil

250g (8 oz) chopped fresh tomatoes

Preparation time: 15 minutes plus soaking time

Cooking time: 1 hour 30 minutes

1. Wash dhal in two or three changes of water and soak in warm water for 3-4 hours. Drain the dhal and discard the water.

2. If using fresh spinach, take off leaves from the stalks, wash in 2 or 3 changes of water. Put in a large bowl with plenty of water and soak for 1 minute, leaving the silt to settle to the bottom. Gently remove the leaves and finely chop on a board or blend in a food processor.

3. Put the water into a pan, add the dhal, bring to the boil and simmer for 40 minutes or until the dhal has softened. Add more water if needed. Drain the dhal and keep to one side. Discard the water.

4. Put the yogurt in a bowl, add salt, red chilli powder and turmeric and using a whisk, mix well.

5. Put the garlic and ginger in the oil in a karahi or saucepan. Fry for 1 minute until the mixture changes colour. Add the spinach, tomatoes and yogurt mixture. Bring to the boil. Stir from time to time and simmer, covered, for 20 minutes, or until spinach is well cooked. If any liquid remains, boil, uncovered, on medium heat until the excess evaporates and the oil separates out. Add the drained dhal and mix once.

Serve with plain rice, chapattis, and marrow raita.

Suitable for freezing.

Balti Maash Dhal

SERVES 4

This popular dry dhal dish, known as 'maash ki khadi dhal', should be 'al dente' and not overcooked and mushy. It is recommended that you use a non-stick pan rather than a karahi for this dish. Cooking skills of new brides are tested on how well they make this dhal which is eaten with slices of onion, Indian radish and wild carrots.

250g (8 oz) urad dhal
water
1 teaspoon salt
½ teaspoon red chilli powder
¼ teaspoon ground turmeric
1 tablespoon tomato purée
2 tablespoons ghee or 4 table spoons corn oil
1 tablespoon finely sliced onion
1 tablespoon finely sliced or grated fresh root ginger
1 sliced fresh green chilli (optional)
2 tablespoons chopped fresh coriander
1 teaspoon Balti garam masala

Preparation time: 10 minutes plus soaking time
Cooking time: 25 minutes

1. Wash the dhal in two or three changes of water and soak in warm water for 30 minutes or more. Strain and discard the water.
2. Put the dhal in a non-stick pan. Add enough water for the level to be just above the dhal. Add the salt, red chilli powder, turmeric and tomato purée. Stir once and simmer, covered, on very low heat for 15 minutes or until the dhal is 'al dente'. Use a wooden spoon to stir very gently once or twice during the cooking. If more water is needed add a tablespoon at a time. Put into a shallow serving dish.
3. In a small frying pan heat the ghee or oil, add the onion and ginger and once they turn brown remove from the heat and pour over the dish. Do not stir. Garnish with sliced fresh chilli if liked, fresh coriander and garam masala.

Serve with a twist of fresh lemon, slices of Indian radish, onion and chapattis or nans.

Suitable for freezing. Once thawed, re-heat dhal in a microwave or under the grill on a low setting to avoid it breaking up.

Prappu
SERVES 2

*P*rappu is a very special dish of Baltistan and is eaten as a full meal. Instead of making the pastry for this dish you can use fresh or dried pasta cooked to the manufacturer's instructions.

For the pastry:
250 g (8 oz) plain white or
  wholemeal flour
180ml (6 fl oz) water or
  enough to bind the flour
flour for dusting

For the paste:
125g (4 oz) shelled walnuts
1 teaspoon ground fresh
  green chillies or ¹/₂ teaspoon
  red chillies (decrease or
  increase to personal taste)
4 tablespoons fresh coriander
  leaves
1 teaspoon salt
60g (2 oz) onion
4 cloves of garlic

3.5 litres (6 pints) water

Preparation time: 15 minutes plus 30 minutes resting time
Cooking time: 20 minutes

1. Mix together the flour and water and knead for 5 minutes until a firm dough is formed. Divide mixture into two, shape roughly into balls and set aside for 30 minutes.
2. Take one of the balls, knead for 5 minutes until smooth and elastic. Roll out on a floured board until 5mm (¹/₄ inch) or thinner. Use a sharp knife to cut into 5cm (2 inch) long strips. Cut diagonally into 5cm (2 inch) diamond shapes. Arrange, with a sprinkling of flour, on a large flat plate. Repeat with the second ball of flour until all the pastry has been cut into pieces.
3. Put the walnuts, fresh chillies, coriander, salt, onion and garlic into a food processor or blender and process to a fine paste. Set aside.
4. Put the water in a large pan and bring to the boil. Allow to simmer. Add the pieces of pastry to the boiling water. Stir once and let the mixture simmer for 10-12 minutes or until the pieces are cooked. Drain in a colander.
5. Put the cooked pastry pieces into a serving dish, add the walnut paste and toss well together.

Serve on its own.

Unsuitable for freezing.

Prappu

Vegetable Dishes and Dhals

Balti Potato
(Balti Aloo)
SERVES 4-5

*P*otatoes are used in a variety of dishes and as Baltistan is a poor region, a lot of people eat potatoes almost four times a week. Sometimes other vegetables are added for variety. This is one of the most popular dishes.

4 tablespoons oil
1 teaspoon cumin seeds
500g (1 lb) potatoes, cut into
   5mm ($^1/_4$ inch) thick slices
$^1/_2$-1 teaspoon red chilli powder
$^1/_4$ teaspoon ground turmeric
1 teaspoon salt
1 teaspoon ground coriander
250g (8 oz) fresh chopped
   tomatoes or 200g (7 oz)
   canned crushed tomatoes
6 tablespoons chopped fresh
   coriander
2 sliced fresh green chillies
   (optional)
1 teaspoon Balti garam masala

Preparation time: 10 minutes
Cooking time: 15 minutes

1. Heat the oil in a karahi or non-stick pan. Add the cumin and once this sizzles, add the sliced potatoes, red chilli powder, turmeric, salt and ground coriander. Mix well, then add the tomatoes.
2. Cover tightly with a lid and cook on a very low heat for 10 minutes or until potatoes are tender. Cooking times will vary with the type of potato used. Stir carefully during the cooking process using a wooden spoon to toss rather than mix the potato slices.
3. Add fresh coriander, chillies, if liked and garam masala.

Serve with chapattis or puris with natural yogurt or salad raita.

Unsuitable for freezing.

Balti Dhal Haleem

SERVES 4-6

Haleem is a very popular dish all over Pakistan and is a favourite roadside speciality. It is a mixture of various dhals, some rice and porridge oats all cooked in one large pot with chicken or lamb. It is sometimes eaten on its own with a spoon as a snack but at other times it is eaten with a nan as a complete meal. As meat is scarce in Baltistan it is omitted in their version of the recipe.

90g (3 oz) urad/mash dhal
90g (3 oz) moong dhal
90g (3 oz) channa dhal
90g (3 oz) masoor dhal
60g (2 oz) long grain rice
150g (5 oz) porridge oats
water
60ml (2 fl oz) milk (optional)
1 teaspoon salt
1 teaspoon red chilli powder
½ teaspoon ground turmeric
juice of one fresh lime
2.5cm (1 inch) piece fresh root
   ginger, grated
2 tablespoons ghee or unsalted
   butter or 3 tablespoons
   corn oil
30g (1 oz) onion, finely sliced
   into rings
1 teaspoon whole cumin seeds

Preparation time: 15 minutes plus soaking time
Cooking time: 50 minutes

1. Spread out the dhals and the rice on a large tray, pick out and discard any stones. Mix all the dhals, rice and oats in a large bowl, then wash in three or four changes of water. Soak overnight in water and milk.

2. Drain the dhal mixture in a sieve and discard the water. Put the dhal mixture into a large saucepan. Pour in enough water so that the level is at least 7.5cm (3 inches) above the dhal mixture. Add the salt, red chilli powder and turmeric. Bring the mixture to the boil, half cover the pan with the lid and simmer for 30-40 minutes, or until dhals and rice are cooked to a pulp. Stir from time to time so that the mixture does not stick to the bottom of the pan.

3. Add the lime juice and boil the mixture, uncovered, until it forms a thick broth-like consistency. Remove from the heat and put into a serving dish. Sprinkle over the ginger.

4. Put the ghee or oil in a heavy-based frying pan, add the onion and fry until a dark golden brown. Add the cumin and remove from the heat. Quickly pour this mixture over the dhal haleem in the serving dish. Do not stir as the beauty of the dish is in the silky rich appearance.

Serve on its own or with warm nans.

Suitable for freezing.

Cheese and Peas in Gravy
(Paneer Mattar di Sabzi)
SERVES 4

*A*ll Punjabis love this dish! The addition of this item to any menu turns a simple meal into a really special one. In taste and appearance, it is hard to find a better combination that pleases one and all.

90ml (3 fl oz) corn oil
200g (7 oz) paneer, cut in 2.5cm (1 inch) cubes (see page 11)
1 small onion, approx. 125g (4 oz), grated
2 cloves of garlic, peeled and finely chopped
1 teaspoon cumin seeds
1 teaspoon ground dried red chillies
$\frac{1}{2}$ teaspoon ground turmeric
salt, to taste
1 tablespoon tomato purée
150g (5 oz) fresh or thawed frozen peas
500ml (16 fl oz) water
$\frac{1}{2}$ teaspoon Indian garam masala

Preparation time: 30 minutes
Cooking time: 30 minutes

1. Put the oil in a deep heavy-based saucepan and place on a medium heat. Fry the paneer cubes until light golden in colour. Drain and set aside.
2. In the same pan, fry the onions until light golden in colour and then add the garlic. Fry for about 30 seconds and add the cumin seeds. Fry for 1 minute and stir in the ground red chillies, turmeric and salt. Reduce the heat, fry for 30 seconds and add the tomato purée. Cook for 1 minute.
3. Add the peas and after frying for 1 minute, increase the heat and stir in the water. Bring to the boil, cover tightly, reduce the heat and cook until the peas are tender and the gravy begins to thicken.
4. Add the fried paneer and mix gently. Cover and simmer on a low heat for 3-5 minutes.
5. Put in a serving dish and sprinkle with garam masala.

Serve with any Indian bread.

Suitable for freezing.

Cheese and Peas in Gravy

Vegetable Dishes and Dhals

Spicy Courgettes
(Tooriyan)
SERVES 4

*T*he Punjabis delight in preparing simple dishes and this recipe is simplicity itself! The delicate flavour of courgettes is enhanced with ginger and the whole dish is deceptively easy to make.

500g (1 lb) courgettes
90ml (3 fl oz) ghee
1 small onion, approx.
   90g (3 oz), sliced
15g ($^1/_2$ oz) fresh root ginger,
   peeled and chopped
2 fresh green chillies, chopped
90g (3 oz) fresh tomatoes,
   chopped
$^1/_2$ teaspoon ground turmeric
$^1/_4$ teaspoon ground dried red
   chillies
salt, to taste
60ml (2 fl oz) water

Preparation time: 15 minutes
Cooking time: 20 minutes

1. Peel and cut the courgettes into 5 mm ($^1/_4$ inch) thick slices.
2. Put the ghee into a deep heavy-based saucepan and place on a high heat. Add the courgettes, onions, ginger and chillies to the pan. Cook for 1-2 minutes.
3. Add the tomatoes, turmeric, ground red chillies and salt to the mixture in the pan.
4. Pour in the water and mix everything well. Cover and bring to the boil. Reduce the heat and cook for about 15 minutes or until the vegetables are tender and all the juices are absorbed. Keep stirring from time to time to stop the mixture from sticking to the base of the pan. When the mixture is semi-dry in appearance, put into a dish and serve.

Serve with nans.

Suitable for freezing.

Spinach with Cheese
(Palak Paneer)
SERVES 4

Many of the best-loved vegetarian Punjabi dishes are the ones where paneer is combined with a vegetable. This combination of spinach and paneer is not only highly nutritious, but is a splendid blend of taste, texture and flavour.

90ml (3 fl oz) ghee

1 small onion, approx. 90g (3 oz), sliced

30g (1 oz) fresh root ginger, peeled and chopped

2 cloves of garlic, peeled and crushed

3 fresh green chillies, chopped

90g (3 oz) tomatoes, skinned and chopped

$^1/_2$ teaspoon ground turmeric

$^1/_2$ teaspoon ground dried red chillies

salt, to taste

750g (1$^1/_2$ lb) fresh spinach, cooked or 500g (1 lb) frozen spinach, thawed

125ml (4 fl oz) milk

250ml (8 fl oz) water

180g (6 oz) paneer cubes about 2.5 cm (1 inch) in size (see page 11)

1 tablespoon thick double cream

Preparation time: 30 minutes

Cooking time: 30 minutes

1. Put the ghee in a heavy-based pan and place on a high heat.

2. Fry the onions until they are light golden in colour. Add the ginger, garlic, and chillies and fry for 1 minute. Add the tomatoes to the pan and cook until tender and well blended. Reduce the heat.

3. Stir in the turmeric, ground red chillies and salt and fry for 30 seconds.

4. Purée the spinach in a liquidiser or food processor. Add the spinach to the hot mixture in the pan and fry for 4-5 minutes. Pour in the milk and water. Bring to the boil, reduce the heat, cover and cook for about 10 minutes or until the mixture is well blended.

5. Add the paneer cubes and mix gently. Cover and simmer for a further 3-4 minutes.

6. Remove from the heat and transfer to a serving dish. Pour the cream on top and mix lightly.

Serve hot with nans or Tandoori Chapatti.

Unsuitable for freezing.

Gram Flour Dumplings in Yogurt Sauce
(Kadhi Kashmiri)
SERVES 4-5

This recipe is a Kashmiri version of Kadhai. Mustard oil and asafoetida give it a distinctive flavour.

For the Pakoras:
150g (5 oz) gram (chick-pea)
   flour
salt to taste
$^1/_4$ -$^1/_2$ teaspoon chilli powder
$^1/_4$ -$^1/_2$ teaspoon whole cumin
   seeds
a pinch of bicarbonate of soda
a pinch of asafoetida, mixed
   with a little water
about 125ml (4 fl oz) warm
   water for mixing
oil or mustard oil for frying

For the Kadhi:
60ml (2 fl oz) natural yogurt,
   mixed with 500ml (16 fl oz)
   water
30g (1 oz) gram (chick-pea)
   flour
1 teaspoon salt or to taste
$^1/_2$ teaspoon chilli powder
$^1/_2$ teaspoon ground turmeric
1 litre (32 fl oz) water
1 tablespoon oil or mustard oil
a pinch of asafoetida
1 teaspoon cumin seeds
1 teaspoon sugar
1 tablespoon fresh mint leaves,
   chopped
2 green chillies, deseeded and
   chopped

Preparation time: 30 minutes
Cooking time: 50 minutes

1. To make the pakoras, mix the gram flour with the salt, chilli powder, cumin seeds, bicarbonate of soda and asafoetida water. Add warm water and mix well until it forms a thick batter.
2. Heat the oil in a wok or deep frying pan. If using mustard oil, heat the oil to smoking point to eliminate the pungency and retain a sweet flavour. Allow to cool and deep fry marble-sized pieces of pakora batter, on a medium heat, until golden brown. Drain on kitchen paper and set aside.
3. For the Kadhi, mix the yogurt-water with the gram flour, whisking well to make sure that there are no lumps. Add the salt, chilli powder, turmeric, and water and whisk well.
4. Heat the oil, add the asafoetida, cumin seeds and the yogurt-water mixture and continue whisking until it starts to boil. Cover and leave on a low heat to simmer for 20 minutes, stirring occasionally.
5. Add the sugar, mint and green chillies and cook for 10 minutes. The consistency should be like a thick soup. Stir in the pakoras and simmer on a low heat until the pakoras are soft.

Serve with white rice.

Unsuitable for freezing.

Gram Flour Dumplings in Yogurt Sauce with rice.

Black Lentils
(Mandira)
SERVES 4-6

*L*entils are a staple food in India and highly nutritious, especially black lentils. Kashmiris use mustard oil for this particular recipe as it gives it that extra special flavour, however any other oil can be substituted. For a more exotic taste mix 250ml (8 fl oz) single cream with 250ml (8 fl oz) yogurt and 60g (2 oz) raisins and add instead of the yogurt.

400g (14 oz) black urad dhal, (whole black lentils)
6 tablespoons mustard oil or any other oil
a pinch of asafoetida
1 tablespoon whole cumin seeds
2 medium onions, sliced
4-6 cloves garlic, minced
2.5cm (1 inch) piece fresh root ginger, peeled and grated
2 tablespoons tomato purée
1 teaspoon ground coriander
$\frac{1}{2}$ teaspoon chilli powder
2 green chillies, chopped (optional)
salt to taste
500ml (16 fl oz) natural yogurt, beaten well

Preparation time: 30 minutes plus 4-6 hours soaking time
Cooking time: 1 hour

1. Wash and soak the dhal for 4-6 hours. Drain and boil the dhal in lightly salted water with 1 tablespoon oil, until tender. Drain and reserve the cooking liquid.
2. Heat the mustard oil in a heavy-based pan on a medium heat and allow to smoke for a few seconds. Reduce the heat and allow to cool slightly. (If using other oils, just heat in the usual way.)
3. Add the asafoetida, cumin seeds, sliced onions, garlic and ginger and stir-fry for 4-5 minutes. Add the tomato purée, coriander, chilli powder and green chillies, if used, and continue stir-frying for a few minutes.
4. Add the drained dhal and salt to taste to the mixture. Stir in the yogurt and enough of the reserved cooking liquid to make a smooth sauce. Cook on a low heat for 15-20 minutes until the mixture is thoroughly blended.

Serve hot with any Indian bread.

Suitable for freezing.

Dry White Mushrooms with Chick-peas
(Dhingri Chole)
SERVES 4-6

The forests of Kashmir are carpeted with fields of fat juicy mushrooms and morels. Dhingri is a dried mushroom and the taste is incredible. It is very expensive and is used on special occasions. This recipe uses Chinese dried mushrooms as a substitute, which are readily available from most Oriental grocers.

625g (1¼ lb) canned chick-peas, drained or 200g (7 oz) dried chick-peas, soaked overnight
salt to taste
½ teaspoon bicarbonate of soda
10 Chinese dried mushrooms
500ml (16 fl oz) water, for soaking mushrooms
5 tablespoons ghee or oil
2 bunches spring onions, approx. 180-200g (6-7 oz), finely chopped
6 cloves garlic, peeled and ground to a paste
5cm (2 inch) piece fresh root ginger, peeled and ground to a paste
3 large tomatoes, chopped
1 teaspoon ground turmeric
2-3 tablespoons lemon juice
2 teaspoons cumin seeds
1 teaspoon Indian garam masala
½ teaspoon chilli powder
½ teaspoon freshly ground black pepper
1 teaspoon ground cumin
250ml (8 fl oz) water
3 tablespoons fresh coriander leaves

Preparation time: 20 minutes (canned chick-peas) or overnight (raw chick-peas)
Cooking time: 45 minutes

1. If using soaked chick-peas, drain them and cook with a little salt, ½ teaspoon bicarbonate of soda and water in a pressure cooker for 25 minutes or alternatively in a covered pan until soft. Drain.
2. Soak the Chinese mushrooms in the water for about 20 minutes and then boil for 5 minutes. Drain and mince coarsely.
3. Heat the oil in a frying pan and fry the spring onions until brown. Add the garlic and ginger, and fry for a few minutes. Add the tomatoes, turmeric, lemon juice, cumin seeds, garam masala, chilli powder, black pepper and ground cumin and stir-fry until the oil comes to the surface.
4. Add the mushrooms and stir-fry for 1 minute. Add the chick-peas and salt to taste and continue stir-frying. Lower the heat, add the water and simmer, tightly covered, for 10 minutes. Sprinkle with the fresh coriander and serve.

Serve with Nans

Unsuitable for freezing.

RICE

Balti Apricot Rice
SERVES 4-6

A *special Balti regional dish made more often in the winter with dried apricots. The fruit and chicken give it a sweet and savoury taste.*

250g (8 oz) whole dried
  apricots
60g (2 oz) thinly sliced onion
2 tablespoons oil
500g (1 lb) boneless chicken,
  cut in 5cm (2 inch) pieces
1/2 teaspoon ground turmeric
1 teaspoon salt
500g (1 lb) basmati rice,
  soaked in water for
  30 minutes
4 tablespoons butter
1 teaspoon saffron

Preparation time: 15 minutes plus soaking time
Cooking time: 30 minutes

1. Slice apricots lengthways and soak in boiling water for 30 minutes, then drain. Remove the stones.
2. Add the onion to the oil in a large frying pan and sauté for 1 minute. Add the chicken pieces, turmeric and salt. Mix well and simmer, uncovered, for 7-10 minutes on medium heat or until chicken pieces are cooked. Dry off any excess liquid, uncovered, on full heat.
3. Cook the rice and then drain and divide into 3 portions.
4. Melt butter in frying pan, add the apricots and fry for 1 minute on full heat. Add the saffron, reduce heat to low and stir for 30 seconds. Remove from the heat.
5. In a large ovenproof dish, put a layer of rice to cover the bottom, follow this with a layer of all the chicken, then another layer of rice, followed by a layer of all the apricot mixture and a final layer of rice.
6. Heat in a preheated oven at 180°C, 350°F, Gas Mark 4 for about 15 minutes.

Serve with natural yogurt flavoured with salt, black pepper and roasted cumin seeds.

Unsuitable for freezing.

Previous pages: Balti Pilao (p.101) and Balti Apricot Rice

Balti Pilao
SERVES 4-6

*T*his dish originates from Afghanistan and is made on special occasions such as feasts or weddings. The carrots and raisins provide a sweetish taste and sometimes boiled chick-peas are also added.

For the stock:
500g (1 lb) leg or shoulder of lamb with bones, cut into 7.5cm (3 inch) pieces
1 tablespoon salt
1.7 litres (3 pints) water

Spice bag:
Two 5cm (2 inch) sticks cassia
6 whole cloves
1 teaspoon black peppercorns
1 tablespoon cumin seeds
1 tablespoon coriander seeds
4-5 whole garlic cloves
125g (4 oz) coarsely chopped onion

6 tablespoons corn oil
90g (3 oz) finely sliced onion
1 tablespoon cumin seeds
Two 5 cm (2 inch) sticks cassia
4 whole cloves
1 teaspoon black peppercorns
500g (1 lb) basmati rice
500g (1 lb) carrots, cut in thin sticks
90g (3 oz) raisins, soaked in water for 3 hours

Preparation time: 20 minutes
Cooking time: 1 hour 20 minutes

1. Put the meat in a large pan, add the salt and water. Put all the spices for the spice bag in a square of muslin or use a piece of J-cloth. Tie up and add to the pan. Bring to the boil and simmer, covered, for 50 minutes or until the meat is cooked.
2. Remove and discard the spice bag. Using a slotted spoon, remove all meat pieces and put into a bowl. Save the stock in a separate bowl.
3. Put the oil and sliced onion into a large pan, fry gently until very, very, dark brown - almost burnt. Quickly add 150ml (^{1}/4 pint) of the lamb stock to stop the onion from browning any further. Add the cumin, cassia, cloves and peppercorns. Fry for 1 minute and add the meat. Stir-fry meat for 5-10 minutes or until the meat is brown. Measure 850ml (1^1/2 pints) stock and add to the meat.
4. Bring to the boil, add the rice and carrots and simmer, uncovered, on medium heat for 10 minutes or until all excess liquid has nearly evaporated. Pile the drained raisins on top of the rice and cover with a layer of foil to overlap sides of the pan. Cover tightly with the lid and keep on the lowest heat setting for 10 minutes. Alternatively, put into a preheated oven at 170°C, 325°F, Gas Mark 3 for 15 minutes.

Serve with natural yogurt thinned with milk.

Unsuitable for freezing.

Rice

101

Balti Biryani
SERVES 6-8

*A*nother *favourite dish for weddings and Idd, the main festival of Baltistan. This is one of the few rice dishes eaten with more than a raita. For example it can be served with Balti chicken, Yellow Balti Meat or Balti Korma.*

500g (1 lb) basmati rice
1 teaspoon saffron
3 tablespoons warm milk
500g (1 lb) neck of lamb, cut in
    5cm (2 inch) pieces
1.15 litres (2 pints) water
1 tablespoon salt
10cm (4 inch) piece cassia bark
1 teaspoon black peppercorns
125g (4 oz) diced onion
4 garlic cloves, peeled
4 tablespoons ghee or 8 table
    spoons oil
8 green cardamom pods
8 whole cloves
8 tablespoons natural low fat
    yogurt
1 teaspoon ground mace
1 teaspoon ground nutmeg

Preparation time: 15 minutes plus soaking time
Cooking time: 1 hour

1. Wash the rice in two or three changes of water and then soak for 30 minutes in warm water. Drain and discard the water. Soak the saffron in milk for 30 minutes.
2. Put the lamb into a large pan and add the water, salt, cassia, peppercorns, onion and garlic. Bring to the boil and simmer, covered, for 40 minutes.
3. Remove the meat from the stock and set aside. Strain the stock and set aside.
4. Put the ghee or oil in a large pan and add the cardamoms and cloves. When spices start to spit add the yogurt. Simmer, uncovered, stirring from time to time until the liquid has evaporated and the mixture is thick.
5. Add the meat, stir on a high heat for 5-10 minutes or until brown. Add 1 litre (1³/₄ pints) of the stock. Bring to the boil.
6. Add the rice, mace and nutmeg and bring to the boil. Simmer, covered, on medium heat for 12 minutes or until the mixture is nearly dry. Make a hollow in the middle of the rice using a small bowl. Pour the milk and saffron into this hollow. Cover the rice with a layer of foil, overlapping the sides of the pan, then tightly cover with a lid and cook on a low heat for 10 minutes. Using a fork gently mix the plain rice with the saffron rice.

Serve with Chicken Korma and a raita.

Unsuitable for freezing.

Balti Biryani

Balti Plum Rice

SERVES 4-6

*T*he dried plums in Baltistan are sour, fruity and delicious but rather different from the dried plums available here. They are made into chutneys and sometimes used in cooking. In this country they can be purchased from an Asian grocer and will be marked 'Alu Bukhara'. If you use dried plums (prunes) from a supermarket, then your dish may be slightly sweet as they are not as sour as their Balti counterparts. It may be more convenient to use tamarind concentrate instead.

150g (5 oz) dried plums or 2 tablespoons tamarind concentrate
500g (1 lb) basmati rice
60g (2 oz) thinly sliced onion
3 tablespoons cooking oil
1 teaspoon ground fresh root ginger
1 teaspoon ground fresh garlic
500g (1 lb) boneless chicken, cut in 5cm (2 inch) pieces
1 teaspoon salt
600ml (1 pint) water

Preparation time: 10 minutes plus soaking time
Cooking time: 40 minutes

1. Soak the plums in boiling water for 30 minutes then drain. Wash the rice in two or three changes of water and soak in warm water for 30 minutes. Drain and discard the water.
2. Place the onions and oil in a karahi or large frying pan and sauté for 1 minute. Add the ginger and garlic and fry the mixture for 1 minute or until it starts to brown.
3. Add the chicken pieces and salt and cook on high heat for 1 minute, then turn down to medium and cook, covered, for 7 minutes or until the chicken is just tender.
4. Add the drained plums or tamarind concentrate to chicken mixture and stir well. Dry off all excess liquid by cooking, uncovered, for about 5 minutes.
5. Add the water, bring mixture to the boil then add the drained rice. Simmer, covered, on medium heat for 10 minutes or until the water is almost absorbed.
6. To finish cooking the dish, either reduce the heat to an absolute minimum or use a heat diffuser. Cover the pan tightly and cook for 15 minutes. Alternatively, put in a preheated oven at 180°C, 350°F, Gas Mark 4 for 15 minutes.

Serve with any raita.

Unsuitable for freezing.

Plain Boiled Rice
SERVES 4-6

*T**he following recipe will result in fluffy, white, long and separate rice grains. Use a large pan with plenty of water. If you increase the quantity of rice, then reduce boiling time by 2 minutes.*

500g (1 lb) basmati rice
1.7 litres (3 pints) water
1 teaspoon lemon juice
1 teaspoon salt
1 tablespoon oil or butter

Preparation time: 5 minutes plus soaking time
Cooking time: 10 minutes

1. Wash the rice in two or three changes of water, then soak in warm water for 30 minutes. Drain rice and discard liquid.
2. Put the measured water into a large pan, bring to the boil, add lemon juice and salt. Add the rice, stir once, bring to the boil and keep boiling for 7-8 minutes, or until rice grains are 'al dente'. Drain the rice.
3. Return the rice to the saucepan and add the oil or butter. Cover with a tight lid and cook on the lowest heat setting for 10 minutes. Do not remove the lid during this time. Gently separate the grains using a fork before serving.

Unsuitable for freezing.

Rice

Balti Meatball and Chick-pea Pilao
(Kofta Channa Pilao)
SERVES 4-5

*S*mall meatballs spiced with chilli, coriander and garam masala, cooked with onions, chick-peas and rice – a meal on its own needing only a salad to make it complete.

250g (8 oz) dried chick-peas
1/2 teaspoon bicarbonate of soda
500g (1 lb) basmati rice
500g (1 lb) lamb or beef mince
60g (2 oz) grated onion
1 teaspoon ground fresh green
chillies
2 tablespoons finely chopped
fresh coriander
1 teaspoon salt
1 teaspoon Balti garam masala
1 egg
4 tablespoons oil
60g (2 oz) finely sliced onion
1 teaspoon whole cumin seeds
1 teaspoon salt
600ml (1 pint) water

Preparation time: 30 minutes plus soaking time
Cooking time: 35 minutes

1. Soak the dried chick-peas in plenty of water overnight, then add the bicarbonate of soda and bring to the boil. Cover and simmer for 1 1/2 hours or until chick-peas are soft. Drain.
2. Wash the rice in two or three changes of water, then soak in warm water for 30 minutes. Drain the rice and discard liquid.
3. Put the mince in a deep bowl and add the grated onion, fresh chillies, coriander, salt, garam masala and egg. Mix well. Divide mixture into 12 small balls, 3.5 cm (1 1/2 inch) in diameter.
4. Put the koftas in a non-stick frying pan and cook without oil on a medium heat for 10 minutes or until any excess liquid evaporates.
5. Put the oil in a large pan and add the sliced onion and fry until dark brown. Add the cumin, chick-peas, salt and the koftas. Simmer, covered, for 3 minutes. Add the water and bring to the boil.
6. Stir in the rice, bring to the boil and simmer, uncovered, on medium heat for 10 minutes. Turn heat to the low, put a piece of foil on top of the pan, cover tightly with the lid and cook for 10 minutes.

Serve with natural yogurt or a raita.

Unsuitable for freezing.

Balti Meatball and Chick-pea Pilao and Salad Raita (p.141)

Lamb Pilao
SERVES 5-6

*T*his recipe is common to all the regions and is cooked on special occasions such as Idd and weddings. It is made with meat on the bone so the stock is rich and strong.

500g (1 lb) basmati rice

For the stock:
500g (1 lb) lamb chops or 500g (1 lb) neck of lamb, cut into 5cm (2 inch) pieces
1.7 litres (3 pints) water
125g (4 oz) diced onion
8 whole cloves of garlic, peeled
1 tablespoon salt
1 tablespoon black peppercorns
10cm (4 inch) piece cassia, broken into four
1 tablespoon cumin seeds
1 tablespoon coriander seeds

2 tablespoons oil
60g (2 oz) thinly sliced onion
1 teaspoon whole cumin seeds
6 black peppercorns
2 cinnamon sticks

Preparation time: 20 minutes plus soaking time
Cooking time: 1 hour

1. Wash the rice in two or three changes of water and soak for 30 minutes in warm water. Drain and discard the water.
2. Put the lamb into a pan, add the water, onion, garlic, salt, black peppercorns, cassia, cumin and coriander. Bring to the boil and simmer, covered, for 50 minutes or until the meat is cooked.
3. Remove the meat pieces with a slotted spoon and put into a bowl. Strain the stock mixture, saving the stock and discarding the rest.
4. Put the oil and sliced onion in a large pan and fry until dark brown. Reduce heat to lowest setting and add the cumin, peppercorns and cinnamon. Increase heat and add the meat pieces. Fry, uncovered, for 5-7 minutes or until meat is brown.
5. Measure 850ml (1½ pints) of stock. If there is not enough stock make up with water. Pour into the pan with the meat and bring to the boil, add the drained rice and stir once. Cook, uncovered, on medium heat for 15 minutes or until the water has nearly all been absorbed. Reduce heat to the lowest setting and cook for 10-15 minutes.

Serve on its own with a salad or raita. At feasts it is served with Balti Chicken, Salt Meat or Balti Chops.

Unsuitable for freezing.

Balti All-in-One Rice
(Murgh Chawal)
SERVES 4-6

The Balti people have found a short cut in preparing rice and curry. They make the curry, add the rice, cook the two together and then eat with natural yogurt and salad or yogurt raita.

500g (1 lb) basmati rice
2 tablespoons oil
250g (8 oz) finely sliced onion
1 tablespoon salt
1 tablespoon ground fresh garlic
1 teaspoon ground fresh green chillies
250g (8 oz) chopped fresh tomatoes
500g (1 lb) boneless chicken, cut in small pieces
1 teaspoon Balti garam masala
850ml (1½ pints) water

Preparation time: 15 minutes plus soaking time
Cooking time: 30 minutes

1. Wash the rice in 2 or 3 changes of water and soak in warm water for 30 minutes. Drain and discard the water.
2. Put the oil in a pan, add the onion and sauté for 1 minute. Add the salt, garlic and fresh chillies and stir well. Cook on medium heat for 3 minutes. Add the tomatoes and cook, uncovered, on medium heat for 5 minutes or until excess liquid evaporates.
3. Add the chicken pieces and garam masala. Cook, covered, on medium heat for 10 minutes, or until the chicken is tender. Stir once or twice with a wooden spoon.
4. Add the water, bring to the boil and then add the rice. Stir once with a wooden spoon and cook, covered, on medium heat for 7-10 minutes until the water is almost absorbed.
5. Place a piece of foil over the top of the pan and cover tightly with the lid. Cook on the lowest heat setting, or use a heat diffuser, for 15 minutes or until rice is fully cooked. Don't be tempted to open the lid or stir during this 'dhum' process.
6. Slowly stir the cooked rice with a fork. Serve using a saucer instead of a spoon to transfer the rice onto a large flat platter, as this will keep the rice grains whole.

Serve with natural yogurt and a fresh green salad.

Unsuitable for freezing.

Rice

SNACKS

Minced Chicken Kebab
(Reshami Kebab)
SERVES 4

A rather special Kebab which is not commonly sold by street vendors in India, but certain eating establishments in Punjab do specialise in them. This Minced Chicken Kebab simply melts in the mouth and is a real treat for the taste buds.

750g (1½ lb) minced uncooked chicken

1 teaspoon ground black pepper

salt, to taste

1 teaspoon garam masala

30g (1 oz) ground cashew nuts or ground almonds

30g (1 oz) fresh root ginger, peeled and grated

4 fresh green chillies, finely chopped

3 tablespoons fresh coriander leaves, finely chopped

2-3 drops yellow food colouring

1 egg

a little ghee for basting

Preparation time: 30 minutes
Cooking time: 15 minutes

1. Put the mince in a bowl and add the pepper, salt, garam masala and ground cashew nuts or almonds. Add the ginger, chillies, coriander and food colouring.

2. Whisk the egg lightly and add to the mixture.

3. Blend the mixture gently. Cover and leave for about 10 to 15 minutes. Preheat the oven to 180°C, 350°F, Gas Mark 4.

4. Divide the mixture into 8 portions.

5. Take a thick skewer, lightly oil your palm and press and spread each portion along the length of the skewer making a long kebab of about 10cm (4 inches). Rotating the skewer whilst pressing the mixture helps to make an even and smooth shaped kebab.

6. Place on a wire rack over a baking tin and roast in the oven for 8-10 minutes. Baste with the ghee and turn the kebabs once or twice so they brown on all sides.

Serve immediately with fresh salad and a chutney.

Unsuitable for freezing.

Previous pages: Minced Chicken Kebab, Chicken Tikka (p. 113) and green mango chutney

Chicken Tikka
(Kukkad de Tikke)
SERVES 4

*C*hicken, which is also known as 'Kukkad' in Punjabi language is no doubt the favourite fare of non-vegetarians. These sizzling and succulent chicken tikkas roasting in a hot tandoor have an aroma that is hard to resist and are surprisingly easy to make.

60g (2 oz) natural yogurt

4 cloves of garlic, peeled and finely chopped

45g (1¹/₂ oz) fresh root ginger, peeled and grated

4 fresh green chillies, finely chopped

¹/₄ teaspoon ground black pepper

¹/₄ teaspoon ground dried red chillies

salt, to taste

¹/₂ teaspoon ground cumin seeds

large pinch of ground nutmeg

1 teaspoon fresh chopped mint, optional

3 tablespoons finely chopped fresh coriander leaves, optional

2 tablespoons of lemon juice

2-3 drops of yellow food colouring or 1 teaspoon ground turmeric

2 tablespoons gram (chick-pea) flour

about 750g (1¹/₂ lb) chicken breast, boned, skinned and cubed

Preparation time: 20 minutes, plus marinating
Cooking time: 15 minutes

1. Put the yogurt in a large bowl and whisk it lightly. Add the garlic, ginger and chillies and mix together.
2. Add the pepper, ground red chillies, salt, cumin, nutmeg, mint and coriander (if used), lemon juice, food colouring (or turmeric) and gram flour to the yogurt and mix thoroughly.
3. Put the chicken into the marinade mixture, cover and leave for at least 3-4 hours.
4. Preheat the oven to 180°C, 350°F, Gas Mark 4. Place the chicken pieces and the marinade in a baking tin, taking care not to cram them too closely and roast for about 15-20 minutes.
5. Just before serving, baste them with the juices left in the tray and grill them for 1-2 minutes under a preheated grill, keeping the tray quite near to the flame to get the slightly 'charred' look which roasting in a tandur would have given. Baste with a little oil if the pieces look too dry and grill for a few seconds.

Serve hot with any chutney or simply squeeze on a little lemon juice and serve as a snack or as part of a main meal.

Suitable for freezing. Use fresh chicken and freeze the marinated pieces (up to stage 4) and finish off the cooking after defrosting.

Snacks

Fish Kebabs
(Machi de Kebab)
SERVES 4

*T*his dish is good to make when giving a cocktail or drinks party. They are *scrumptious served with any chutney or even tomato ketchup, and are a rewarding treat for very little effort.*

500g (1 lb) cod steaks or any
  firm flesh white fish
1 teaspoon lemon juice
1/2 teaspoon ground black
  pepper
Salt, to taste
2 cloves of garlic, peeled and
  crushed
30g (1 oz) onion, finely
  chopped
3 fresh green chillies, finely
  chopped
2 tablespoons fresh coriander
  leaves, finely chopped
2 slices white bread made into
  fresh breadcrumbs
1 egg
oil for deep frying

Preparation time: 20 minutes
Cooking time: 10 minutes

1. Steam the fish lightly and remove any skin and all the bones. Flake the pieces gently with a fork. Put the fish in a bowl and add the lemon juice, pepper and salt.
2. Add the garlic, onion, chillies, coriander and breadcrumbs to the fish and mix gently.
3. Beat the egg lightly, add to the mixture and bind it well. Divide the mixture into walnut-sized balls.
4. Heat the oil in a kadhai or deep frying pan and on a medium heat, fry the fish kebabs (balls) until golden brown. Drain on absorbent kitchen paper.

Serve hot with chutney.

Unsuitable for freezing.

Fish Kebabs and chutney

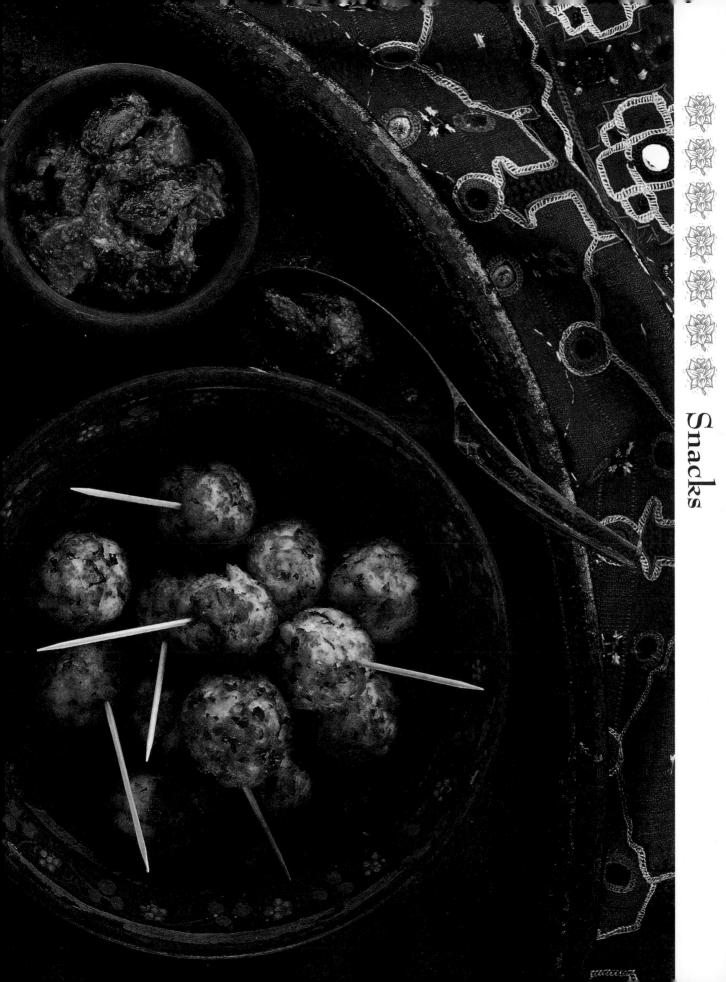

Snacks

Minced Lamb on Skewers
(Keeme di Seekhan)
SERVES 4

*T*he word 'Seekh' means 'a skewer' and kebabs grilled on a seekh are termed as 'seekhan' in Punjab. The origins of such cooking may lie in the Middle East but over time it has become one of the methods used for Indian cooking.

4 cloves
8 black peppercorns
1 tablespoon coriander seeds
1 teaspoon cumin seeds
1 tablespoon white poppy seeds
30g (1 oz) fresh root ginger, peeled and grated
30g (1 oz) onion, peeled and chopped
2 tablespoons fresh coriander leaves, finely chopped
2 tablespoons natural yogurt
1 tablespoon lemon juice
1 tablespoon mustard oil
1 tablespoon dried fenugreek leaves, crumbled
salt, to taste
750g (1/2 lb) minced lamb
1 egg, lightly beaten
a little ghee for basting

Preparation time: 1 hour
Cooking time: 15 minutes

1. Place a heavy-based frying pan on a high heat and dry roast the cloves, peppercorns, coriander, cumin and poppy seeds. Stir until they are evenly browned. Remove and grind to a powder.
2. Put the ginger, onion, and coriander in a bowl, and combine with the ground spices, yogurt, lemon juice, mustard oil, fenugreek leaves and salt.
3. Add the lamb and mix thoroughly. Put the mixture into a food processor, add the egg and process until well blended. Cover and leave to stand for at least 30 minutes.
4. Preheat the oven to 180°C, 350°F, Gas mark 4. Divide the mixture into 12. Take a thick skewer, lightly oil your palm and press and spread each portion along the length of a skewer, making a 13-15cm (5-6 inch) long kebab. Rotating the skewer while pressing the mixture helps to make an even and smooth shaped kebab.
5. Place on a rack over a baking tin and roast for 5-7 minutes in the oven. Turn once during cooking.
6. Just before serving, baste with ghee and put the kebabs under a preheated grill for a few seconds. This will give a slightly 'charred' look which roasting in a tandoor would have given.

Serve the kebabs, removed from the skewers, with fresh salad and nans.

Suitable for freezing.

Pan-fried Liver
(Bhunni Kaleji)
SERVES 4

*T*his recipe can be grilled instead of pan-fried, simply thread the pieces on skewers
and grill under a high heat, turning frequently.

500g (1 lb) lamb's liver, cut in
   5cm (2 inch) pieces
1 tablespoon lemon juice
60g (2 oz) onion, cut up
3 fresh green chillies
1/2 teaspoon ground turmeric
1/2 teaspoon ground dried red
   chillies
salt, to taste
2 tablespoons corn oil
1 teaspoon Indian garam
   masala
1 teaspoon tomato purée
2 tablespoons fresh coriander
   leaves

Preparation time: 15 minutes
Cooking time: 10 minutes

1. Wash the liver and drain thoroughly. Put in a
bowl, sprinkle with lemon juice and set aside.
2. Put the onions, chillies, turmeric, ground red
chillies and salt into a liquidiser and blend.
3. Add the mixture to the liver and mix thoroughly,
coating all the pieces.
4. Heat the oil in a frying pan over a medium heat.
Add the liver and fry for 3-4 minutes. Reduce the
heat and cook until the liver is tender and brown.
5. Add the garam masala, tomato purée and
coriander leaves and fry for a further 2-3 minutes.
Cover and simmer on a very low heat for 2-3
minutes or until the liver is well done. Stir
occasionally to prevent the mixture from sticking to
the pan.

Serve with Indian bread, or simply use as a topping
for mini-toasts and serve as a snack.

Unsuitable for freezing.

Home-made Cheese Tikka
(Paneer de Tikke)
SERVES 4

*T*he 'tandoori' style of cooking lends itself mainly to non-vegetarian dishes. So here is a recipe for a vegetarian 'tikka' that uses paneer, a home-made cheese that does not melt when cooked. For those who do not eat eggs, omit the egg and add 1 more tablespoon each of gram flour and cream.

500g (1 lb) paneer (see page 11)

$^1/_2$ teaspoon ground turmeric

$^1/_2$ teaspoon ground black pepper

1 teaspoon Indian garam masala

$^1/_4$ teaspoon ground mango powder

$^1/_2$ teaspoon dry roasted ground cumin seeds

salt, to taste

1 teaspoon dried fenugreek leaves

2 tablespoons gram (chick-pea) flour

2 tablespoons thick double cream

1 egg, lightly beaten

$^1/_4$ teaspoon ground dried red chillies

Preparation time: 30 minutes
Cooking time: 15 minutes

1. Cut the paneer into pieces 3.5cm (1$^1/_2$ inch) square and 2.5cm (1 inch) thick. Put in a shallow bowl and sprinkle with the turmeric, pepper, garam masala, mango powder, cumin seeds, salt and fenugreek leaves. Toss the paneer gently to coat well with all the spices. Set aside for 15 minutes.
2. In a bowl put gram flour, cream, egg, salt and ground red chillies. Whisk well until a smooth, thick batter is formed. Add the spiced paneer to the batter. Mix gently, coating all the pieces thoroughly. Set aside for 15 minutes.
3. Preheat the oven to 180°C, 350°F, Gas Mark 4. Thread the paneer tikkas on to skewers, leaving spaces in between each piece.
4. Place the skewers on a wire rack over a baking tin and cook in the oven for about 10-12 minutes. Turn them once during cooking.
5. Just before serving, place the tikkas under a hot grill for a few seconds to brown the edges.

Serve hot with any chutney recipe.

Unsuitable for freezing.

Home-made Cheese Tikka with Bread Fritters (p.120) and chutney

Bread Fritters
(Double Roti de Pakode)
SERVES 4

There are many different types of pakodas (fritters) and they are a very simple yet delicious snack food. These are easily made with bread slices.

180g (6 oz) gram (chick-pea)
    flour
$\frac{1}{2}$ teaspoon ground dried red
    chillies
salt, to taste
$\frac{1}{2}$ teaspoon carom seeds,
    optional
2 tablespoons fresh coriander
    leaves, finely chopped
1 tablespoon warm corn oil
water to make batter
about 4 to 6 white medium
    thick bread slices
oil for deep frying

Preparation time: 20 minutes
Cooking time: 10 minutes

1. Sieve the gram flour, ground red chillies and salt into a bowl. Add the carom seeds, (if used) and coriander.
2. A little at a time, pour in the oil with enough water to make a fairly thick, smooth batter of a coating consistency. Cover and set aside for about 10-15 minutes.
3. Cut the bread slices diagonally into triangle shapes. Put the oil in a khadai, or deep frying pan, and place it on a medium heat.
4. Take one half slice at a time and dip it in the batter. Coat thoroughly with batter and deep fry until golden. Keep the heat on medium to low so that the batter has time to cook and does not get brown too quickly.
5. Fry all the slices and drain on absorbent kitchen paper.

Serve hot with any chutney of your liking.

Unsuitable for freezing.

Potato Cutlets
(Aloo di Tikki)
SERVES 4

Street food is enormously popular in India. The street vendor selling Aloo di tikki is the most sought after, especially if he serves a really good chutney to accompany the tikki! Here is a quick and easy way to make them. Aloo di tikki is often made with added cooked minced lamb and you can also try substituting dry cooked lentils instead of peas for a wonderful variation in taste.

500g (1 lb) boiled potatoes, mashed

180g (6 oz) peas, fresh or frozen, cooked

60g (2 oz) onion, finely chopped

30g (1 oz) fresh root ginger, peeled and finely chopped

4 tablespoons fresh coriander leaves, chopped

4 fresh green chillies, chopped

1 teaspoon Indian garam masala

$1/4$ teaspoon ground dried red chillies

salt, to taste

1 tablespoon lemon juice

oil for shallow frying

Preparation time: 30 minutes
Cooking time: 10 minutes

1. Put the potatoes into a bowl and add the peas, onion, ginger, coriander and chillies.
2. Sprinkle in the garam masala, ground red chillies and salt. Add the lemon juice and mix well. Gently knead the whole mixture until everything is well blended.
3. Divide the mixture into 8-10 portions. Roll each into a ball and then press lightly to form a flat, round patty. It is easier to do these against a wet palm. Shape all the 'tikkis' in this way.
4. Heat a griddle or a heavy-based frying pan on a medium heat. Use about 1 or 2 tablespoons of oil to grease the griddle thoroughly. Shallow fry the tikkis, turning them once, until they are golden brown on both sides. Keep adding the oil a little at a time while frying. Drain on absorbent kitchen paper.

Serve with chutney.

Unsuitable for freezing.

Flaky Pastry Savouries
(Mathi)
SERVES 4

*A*ll over India one can see how innovative and enthusiastic people are about 'snack' cuisine. There is a tremendous availability of food to nibble on and one of the more traditional and commonly made among them is 'mathi', a super, slow-fried, crispy savoury.

300g (10 oz) plain white flour
1 teaspoon carom seeds
1 teaspoon black peppercorns,
   roughly crushed
salt, to taste
2 tablespoons corn oil
60ml (2 fl oz) milk
60ml (2 fl oz) water
oil for deep frying

Preparation time: 30 minutes
Cooking time: 30 minutes

1. Sieve the flour into a bowl. Add the carom seeds, peppercorns, and salt and mix well.
2. Pour the oil into the mixture, a little at a time and rub it in well.
3. Mix the milk and water together and add slowly to the flour. Knead to make a stiff dough. Use a little more water if needed. The dough should be smooth but hard.
4. Divide the dough into 12-16 portions. Roll into balls and with a rolling pin, flatten them into round shapes. They should be approx. 2.5mm ($^1/_8$ inch) thick and 6cm ($2^1/_2$ inch) in diameter.
5. With a fork, prick all over the surface of each mathi. Cover with a cloth to prevent them from drying out.
6. Put the oil in a khadai or heavy-based deep pan and place on a medium heat.
7. When the oil is fairly hot, slowly put in the mathis, a few at a time, and fry for about 1 minute or until they come sizzling to the surface of the oil. Reduce the heat to low and fry slowly until they are golden brown. Remove and drain on absorbent kitchen paper.

Serve with green mango pickle or on their own.

Unsuitable for freezing. However they can be stored in an airtight container for up to 4 weeks.

Flaky Pastry Savouries and green mango pickle

Samosas
SERVES 4

*I*f there is one snack that is universally loved across the whole Indian subcontinent, it is the 'samosa'. The Punjabi samosa has its own little touch — the use of pomegranate seeds and its large size! Although they take a little time to make, the end result is always rewarding.

150g (5 oz) plain white flour
pinch of salt
60ml (2 fl oz) corn oil
water to mix
1 quantity of Pea and Potato
   Filling (see opposite)
flour
oil for deep frying

Preparation time: 1 hour
Cooking time: 15 minutes

1. Sieve together the flour and salt into a bowl. Rub in the oil and add enough water to make a stiff but pliable dough. Cover with a damp cloth and leave to rest for 10-15 minutes.
2. Divide the dough into 6 and shape each into a ball. Using a little flour, roll out each ball into a thin round disc approx. 15cm (6 inch) in diameter and cut in half.
3. Make each half into a cone shape, and seal the edges with water. Stuff generously with the pea/potato filling. Moisten the edges and seal the open ends by pressing firmly together.
4. Fill the remaining cones in the same way Cover with a cloth and set aside.
5. Put the oil in a khadai or heavy-based deep pan and place it on a medium heat. Fry the samosas on low to medium heat until they are golden on each side. Remove and drain on absorbent paper.

Serve hot with chutney.

Unsuitable for freezing.

Pea and Potato Filling for Samosas

*T*he fillings used in samosas reflect to some extent the varying regional tastes. Potato Samosas are extremely popular in Punjab, with a minced lamb variety a close runner-up. Other regions use lentils and mixed vegetables as a filling for these 'pastry parcels'.

2 tablespoons ghee

1 teaspoon cumin seeds

15g (½ oz) fresh root ginger, peeled and finely chopped

4 fresh green chillies,chopped

280g (9 oz) potatoes, peeled and cut into 0.5cm (¼ inch) dice

salt to taste

½ teaspoon Indian garam masala

1 teaspoon ground pomegranate seeds

90g (3 oz) frozen peas, thawed

2 tablespoons finely chopped fresh coriander leaves

1. Put the ghee in a pan and place it on a medium heat. Add the cumin seeds and fry them until they begin to splutter and pop.

2. Add the ginger and chillies to the pan and fry for about 30 seconds.

3. Add the potatoes, salt, garam masala and ground pomegranate seeds to the pan. Mix well. Reduce the heat, cover and cook until the potatoes are tender.

4. Add the peas and mix everything well. Cover and cook on low heat until the peas are tender. Both the potatoes and peas should be soft, but not mashed.

5. Add the finely chopped coriander leaves and stir well. Allow the mixture to become cold before using for Samosas.

BREADS, PICKLES AND RAITAS

Chapattis
(Roti)
SERVES 2-3

*C*hapattis are eaten in almost every Indian and Pakistani home and Balti homes are no exception. Chapattis are made of unleavened wholemeal flour called atta or chapatti flour, available from large supermarkets and Asian grocers.

250g (8 oz) chapatti or plain
   wholemeal flour
200ml (7 fl oz) water
approx 200g (7 oz) chapatti or
   wholemeal flour for dusting

Preparation time: 40 minutes
Cooking time: 10 minutes

1. Put the flour in a bowl and gradually add enough water to mix to a stiff dough.
2. Knead for 5 minutes then cover and leave for 30 minutes.
3. Knead for 2 minutes. Heat a tawa, griddle or heavy-based frying pan on a low heat. Shape the dough into 3-4 balls and dip each one into the bowl of dusting flour.
4. Roll out one ball into a round on a flat surface using a rolling pin. Roll it as thin as you can, dusting with flour as necessary.
5. Put the chapatti on to the hot tawa. Cook for 30-40 seconds on medium heat or until it changes colour and brown flecks appear. Turn it over and cook the other side.
 6. Use a clean tea towel to press round all the edges and then in the middle, turn and do the same to the other side. With practice the chapattis will puff up.
7. Cook the remaining chapattis in the same way. Keep, covered, in a tea towel or foil. If left uncovered they will dry out and turn brittle.

Serve immediately, spread with a little butter or ghee if liked.

Suitable for freezing.

Previous pages: Tandoori Chapatti (p.129)
Ginger and Green Chilli Preserve (p.133) and Cauliflower Pickle (p.133)

Tandoori Chapatti
(Tandoori Roti)
SERVES 3

*T*andoori rotis are a cross between a nan and a chapatti and are popular all over the country. They are thicker than chapattis and thinner than nans. People either buy the rotis from the tandoor or take their own kneaded unleavened dough to the tandoor and have them made for a small charge.

250g (8 oz) chapatti flour
125g (4 oz) plain flour
1 teaspoon salt
½ teaspoon bicarbonate of
   soda
300-350ml (10-12 fl oz) water
approx 200g (7 oz) plain flour
   for dusting

Preparation time: 40 minutes
Cooking time: 20 minutes

1. Mix both the flours, bicarbonate of soda and the salt in a bowl.
2. Gradually add the water and mix to form a dough. You may need to adjust the amount of water depending on the texture of the flour. Knead thoroughly on a floured board for 5-10 minutes.
3. Let dough rest for 30 minutes. Divide the dough into 4 or 5 equal portions. Take one portion, dip into the dusting flour and make into a ball. Make all the portions into balls, dip each ball into the flour and set aside.
4. Heat a tawa, griddle or non-stick frying pan on low heat until hot. Switch on grill to full setting. Roll out each ball, into a round of 5cm (¼ inch) thickness, frequently dusting with the flour.
5. Put rolled out roti onto the hot tawa, cook on both sides for 40 seconds or until it changes colour. Use a fish slice and transfer it to the grill rack and grill under full heat for 1-2 minutes or until puffed up and browned all over. Remove and keep in foil or a tea towel to keep them warm and soft.

Serve and eat immediately.

Suitable for freezing.

Puris
SERVES 2

In Baltistan, Puris are mainly eaten with vegetable or dhal dishes. They are made using the same unleavened flour as for the chapattis, but deep fried in hot oil which makes them puff up. They are much smaller than chapattis.

250g (8 oz) chapatti or plain
   wholemeal flour
1 teaspoon salt
1 tablespoon oil
200ml (7 fl oz) water
oil for deep frying
approx 200g (7 oz) chapatti or
   wholemeal flour for dusting

Preparation time: 40 minutes
Cooking time: 15 minutes

1. Put the flour and salt in a deep bowl, mix the oil into the flour with your hands and gradually add enough water to form a stiff dough. You may need slightly less or slightly more water depending on the amount of husk in the flour.
2. Knead for 5 minutes then leave, covered, for 30 minutes to give the flour particles time to absorb the water.
3. Knead for 2 minutes. Put the oil into a karahi or a frying pan and heat on low until hot.
4. Divide the dough into 6 parts, take one part and dip in the dusting flour and shape into a ball. Then roll out to a 5mm ($^1/_4$ inch) thickness, dipping in the dusting flour if required.
5. Lower the puri gently into the hot oil, press down with a slotted spoon and cook for 10 seconds. The puri will puff up. Turn it over and cook the second side for 10 seconds or until golden brown.
6. Remove carefully from oil and save on a large platter lined with kitchen paper. Fry all the puris in the same way and pile in a dish and serve.

Serve with any vegetarian dish.

Suitable for freezing – but they are best eaten freshly made and puffed up.

Nans (p.132) and Puris

Nans

SERVES 3

*N*ans are made with leavened dough and are eaten all over the country. The kneaded dough is either rolled or pulled to a round or tear drop shape and slapped onto the wall of a hot tandoor oven using a specially made hard cushion.

1 tablespoon natural yogurt
1 teaspoon salt
1 teaspoon sugar
1 tablespoon easy-blend dried
  yeast
1 tablespoon melted butter or
  oil
500g (1 lb) self raising flour
hand hot water
bowl of plain flour for dusting

Preparation time: 10 minutes plus 2 hours rising time
Cooking time: 15 minutes

1. Put the yogurt in a bowl, add the salt, sugar, yeast and butter or oil and mix well.
2. Put the flour into a bowl. Add the yogurt mixture and enough warm water to mix to a soft dough. Knead well on a floured board for 5-10 minutes until dough is soft and pliable.
3. Return to the bowl, brush a thin layer of oil on the surface, cover with cling film or a clean tea towel and put in a warm place for 2 hours.
4. Knead the dough and divide into 6-8 equal pieces. Dip each into the dusting flour and shape into balls. Cover with cling film.
5. Preheat the grill. Heat a griddle, tawa or non-stick frying pan on a low heat until hot.
6. Roll out each ball into a round shape 5mm (¼ inch) thick on a lightly floured surface. Prick each nan with a fork 4 or 5 times so it does not puff up into the grill.
7. Pick the nan up, if preferred pull one side to shape into a tear-drop shape, slap onto the hot griddle and cook for 45 seconds or until the bottom side is cooked and has brown flecks.
8. Using a fish slice, transfer the nan to the grill rack. Cook for 1-2 minutes or until golden brown and puffy. Cook the remaining nans in the same way and keep wrapped up in foil or a clean kitchen towel.

Serve warm, brushed with melted butter.

Suitable for freezing.

Cauliflower Pickle
(Gobi Ka Achar)

125g (4 oz) cauliflower, cut into 2.5cm (1 inch) pieces

30g (1 oz) demerara sugar

8 tablespoons white distilled malt vinegar

1 teaspoon coarsely ground dried red chillies

1 teaspoon salt

Preparation time: 8 minutes
Maturing time: 7-10 days

1. Spread out the cauliflower pieces on a flat plate. Microwave for 1 minute or sun dry for 8 hours then cool.
2. Put the sugar and vinegar into a pan, bring to the boil, add the chillies and salt and switch off. Cool slightly.
3. Put the cauliflower pieces into a small glass jar, pour the warm liquid over it and store open, in direct light, for 7-10 days.

Ginger and Green Chilli Preserve

125g (4 oz) fresh root ginger, peeled

60g (2 oz) fresh green chillies

1 teaspoon salt

2 tablespoons lemon juice

2 tablespoons white distilled malt vinegar

Preparation time: 7 minutes
Maturing time: 3-4 days

1. Finely slice the ginger into thin strips against the grain and put into a jar.
2. Slice the chillies lengthways into two leaving the seeds in. Add these to the jar with the ginger.
3. Add the salt, lemon juice and vinegar and mix well. Keep the jar, covered, in the refrigerator. Ready to eat in 4-5 days.

Keeps for 2-3 weeks in the refrigerator.

Mixed Vegetable Pickle
(Sabzi Ka Achar)

This is one pickle where any seasonal vegetables are used. The vegetables chosen for this recipe are readily available in Britain.

250g (8 oz) carrots
250g (8 oz) mooli (white radish)
250g (8 oz) cauliflower
250g (8 oz) turnips
1 teaspoon black mustard seeds
1 teaspoon fenugreek seeds
5 whole cloves
1 teaspoon nigella (onion seeds)
1 tablespoon cumin seeds
125ml (4 fl oz) vegetable oil
1 teaspoon ground fresh root ginger
1 teaspoon ground fresh garlic
1 tablespoon salt
1 teaspoon ground turmeric
180ml (6 fl oz) white distilled malt vinegar
1 teaspoon red chilli powder
1 tablespoon Balti garam masala

Preparation time: 15 minutes
Cooking time: 15 minutes

1. Cut the carrots and mooli into approx. 5cm (2 inch) long sticks. Cut the cauliflower into very small florets and the turnips into small wedges.
2. Place the mustard, fenugreek, cloves, nigella and cumin in a coffee grinder and process for 30 seconds until coarsely ground.
3. Put the oil into a large pan. Add the ginger and garlic, fry on a low heat for 5-7 minutes or until brown. Add all the vegetables, salt and turmeric. Mix once and add the coarsely ground spices. Stir well. Add the vinegar, chilli powder and garam masala.
4. Simmer, uncovered, on a low heat for 5-7 minutes or until vegetables are cooked but still firm. Remove from the heat and cool completely.
5. Place in a large jar and store in the refrigerator.

Keeps for 4-8 weeks in the refrigerator.

Mixed Vegetable Pickle, Lemon Pickle (p.136) and Mango Pickle (p.137)

Lemon Pickle

*L*emons are only available in the summer in Baltistan. so they are pickled in four or five different ways and eaten throughout the year.

6 small unwaxed lemons or
limes
60g (2 ozs) fresh green chillies
125ml (4 fl oz) mustard or
corn oil
1 whole clove garlic, peeled
1 tablespoon fenugreek seeds
1 tablespoon fennel seeds
1 tablespoon salt
1 teaspoon red chilli powder
1 teaspoon ground turmeric

Preparation time: 10 minutes plus soaking time
Maturing time: 5-7 days

1. Wash the lemons or limes and soak in warm water for 8 hours or overnight. Remove from the water and dry with kitchen paper.
2. Cut 3 of the lemons into thin whole slices, 5mm ($^1/_4$ inch) thick and arrange on a flat plate. Either place in direct sunlight for 8 hours or microwave for 2 minutes on full setting. Put aside to cool in a bowl.
3. Squeeze the juice of the 3 remaining lemons and pour onto the slices. Slice chillies in half lengthways and add to the lemons.
4. Put the oil into a pan. Add the peeled garlic and heat on low heat until the garlic turns light brown. Remove from the heat and cool the oil completely.
5. To the cooled oil, add the fenugreek, fennel, salt, red chilli powder and turmeric. Add this mixture to the bowl of lemons and green chillies.
6. Mix well with a wooden spoon. Store in jars. Make sure there is a layer of oil on top of the lemons, to stop the pickle from going mouldy. Keep for 5-7 days to mature.

Keeps for 3-4 weeks.

Mango Pickle
(Aam Ka Achar)

The Baltis have a favourite pickle and that is 'aam ka achar'. According to some of the old cooks, there are 30 different ways of pickling mangoes. Substitute cooking apples if mangoes are not available.

500g (1 lb) raw green mangoes
2 teaspoons salt
1 teaspoon ground turmeric
1 teaspoon crushed dried red chillies
2 tablespoons fennel seeds
2 tablespoons fenugreek seeds
2 tablespoons nigella (onion seeds)
2 tablespoons cumin seeds
2 tablespoons mustard seeds
125ml (4 fl oz) mustard or corn oil
1 whole clove garlic, peeled

Preparation time: 20 minutes
Maturing time: 15 days

1. Wash the mangoes in cold water and dry with kitchen paper. Slice or cut into 5cm (2 inch) long thick slices or into a size of your choice. If the mangoes are 5-10cm (2-4 inches) in size, cut into 4-6 pieces from top to bottom through the seed, . Remove and discard the seed.
2. Place the mangoes into a wide-necked jar. Add the salt, turmeric, red chillies, fennel, fenugreek, nigella, cumin and mustard seeds. Mix well. Keep the bottle in the sun for 4-7 days or on a window-sill in natural light for 10 days. Move the mangoes around once a day with a clean dry spoon.
3. Put the oil into a pan. Add the peeled garlic and heat on low heat until the garlic turns light brown. Remove from the heat and cool the oil completely.
4. Pour the tempered oil over the mixture in the jar making sure that the oil is above the mangoes and spices otherwise the pickle will begin to go mouldy.
5. Store, covered, for a further 7 days on the window-sill, stirring with a clean dry spoon once a day. The mangoes will then soften and be ready to eat.

Eat within 3-4 weeks.

Breads, Pickles and Raitas

Green Apple Pickle

*T*his pickle is made with mangoes in Baltistan but you can use cooking apples which make a lovely alternative.

350g (12 oz) cooking apples
60g (2 oz) fresh green chillies
1 tablespoon fennel seeds
1 tablespoons fenugreek seeds
6 tablespoons vegetable oil
1 tablespoon ground fresh garlic
1 tablespoons cumin seeds
1 tablespoon Balti garam masala
1 tablespoon salt
1 teaspoon ground dried red chillies
1 teaspoon ground turmeric
8 tablespoons white distilled malt vinegar
1 teaspoon citric acid or 2 tablespoons lemon juice

Preparation time: 15 minutes
Cooking time: 10 minutes
Maturing time: 1 day

1. Core and dice the apples into 2.5 cm (1 inch) cubes. Slice green chillies lengthways into two.
2. Coarsely grind fennel and fenugreek seeds in a coffee grinder.
3. Heat the oil in a large pan and add the ground garlic. Cook, uncovered, on medium heat for 2 minutes or until garlic begins to brown. Add the cumin, garam masala, fennel, fenugreek, salt, ground dried red chillies, turmeric, vinegar and citric acid or lemon juice. Stir well and cook on low heat, uncovered, for 2 minutes.
4. Add the apples and green chillies. Stir and cook for 5 minutes or until apples are cooked but still firm. Cool and keep in covered, glass jars.

Keeps well for 2-3 weeks.

Aubergine Raita (p.140) and Green Apple Pickle

Aubergine Raita
(Bengun Raita)
SERVES 8

*B*altis seem to have a special liking for aubergines. When readily available they are dried in the sun and used at a later date, after soaking. They eat chapattis with this dish, especially in the summer months.

125g (4 oz) aubergine
250g (8 oz) natural full fat
  yogurt
$\frac{1}{2}$ teaspoon salt
pinch of ground black pepper
$\frac{1}{2}$ teaspoon finely sliced fresh
  green chillies (optional)
2-4 tablespoons milk
1 tablespoon cumin seeds
1 tablespoon finely sliced onion
1 tablespoon finely sliced fresh
  coriander
$\frac{1}{2}$ teaspoon paprika (optional)

Preparation time: 20 minutes

1. If aubergines are fist size, place whole aubergines under a preheated grill for 4 minutes each side or until brown. If the aubergine is large (e.g. Dutch) then cut into half and grill both sides. Lower gently into cold water. Soak for 5 minutes then take the skin off gently and discard it. Chop up or use a fork to mash the mixture into a coarse pulp.
2. Put the yogurt into a serving dish, add salt, pepper and chillies, if used, and mix well with a fork until smooth. Add 2-4 tablespoons of milk to thin down the yogurt, if needed, and beat well with a fork. Add the cooled aubergine pulp and put in the refrigerator.
3. Heat a frying pan on low heat until hot. Add the cumin, switch off after 30 seconds. Remove and cool.
4. Just before serving, add the onion to the raita and mix, then garnish with fresh coriander and paprika. Take the cumin in the palm of the left hand, bruise with the base of the right hand and sprinkle on the raita.

Serve with vegetarian or meat dishes.

Unsuitable for freezing.

Marrow Raita
(Kadu Raita)
SERVES 8

180g (6 oz) grated kadu (see page 74) or turnip or courgettes
300ml ($^1/_2$ pint) water
250g (8 oz) natural full fat or Greek yogurt
$^1/_2$ teaspoon salt
pinch of red chilli powder
$^1/_2$ teaspoon finely sliced fresh green chillies (optional)
2 tablespoons milk
1 tablespoon finely chopped fresh coriander
1 tablespoon dry roasted cumin seeds

Preparation time: 15 minutes

1. Put the kadu and water into a pan, bring to the boil and simmer for 3 minutes or until kadu is par-cooked. Strain kadu and allow to cool.
2. Put the yogurt into a serving dish, add the salt, red chilli powder, fresh chillies if used and milk. Mix well until smooth. Add cooled kadu and store in the refrigerator.
3. To serve, sprinkle with fresh coriander. Bruise the cumin in your hands and sprinkle over the raita.

Serve with vegetarian and meat dishes.

Unsuitable for freezing.

Salad Raita
SERVES 10

500g (1 lb) low fat natural yogurt
$^1/_2$ teaspoon salt
$^1/_2$ teaspoon ground black pepper
125g (4 oz) cucumber, diced
125g (4 oz) tomatoes, diced
60g (2 oz) onions, diced
2 tablespoons chopped fresh coriander
1 teaspoon Balti garam masala

Preparation time: 10 minutes

1. Place the yogurt in a bowl, add the salt and pepper and beat well with a fork until the yogurt is smooth.
2. Add the salad vegetables and mix once. Garnish with coriander and garam masala.

Unsuitable for freezing.

SWEETS

Sweet Saffron Rice
(Mithe Chawal)
SERVES 4

*D*esserts made with rice are popular in Punjab and this particularly unusual version of rice is a speciality prepared for important occasions.

250g (8 oz) basmati rice
400ml (14 fl oz) water
90g (3 oz) ghee
3 green cardamoms
4 whole cloves
1/2 teaspoon saffron
1 tablespoon hot water
180g (6 oz) sugar
30g (1 oz) sultanas
30g (1 oz) slivered almonds
30g (1 oz) shelled pistachios,
   roughly chopped
2-3 drops rose essence
3-4 silver leaves

Preparation time: 20 minutes
Cooking time: 30 minutes

1. Wash the rice in several changes of water, until the water runs clear. Soak in a bowl with 400 ml (14 fl oz) of water and leave for 15-20 minutes. Drain and reserve the water for cooking the rice later.
2. Put the ghee in a deep heavy-based saucepan and place it on a medium heat. Add the whole cardamoms and cloves and fry until they change colour and begin to splutter.
3. Add the drained rice and fry for 3-4 minutes. Pour in the reserved water and bring to the boil. Reduce the heat and cook until the rice is tender.
4. Add the saffron to the hot water and crush gently. Leave to stand 1-2 minutes.
5. Add the sugar and saffron to the rice and stir until the sugar has dissolved.
6. Preheat the oven to 120°C, 250°F, Gas Mark 1/2 Soak the sultanas in a little hot water for 5 minutes, then drain.
7. Add the sultanas and half the amount of almonds and pistachios to the pan and stir gently. Add the rose essence and mix gently.
8. Transfer the rice to an ovenproof dish, sprinkle with the remaining nuts, cover and bake in the oven for about 15-20 minutes.

Serve hot, decorated with the silver leaves.

Unsuitable for freezing.

Previous pages: Gulab Jamun (p.145) and Sweet Saffron Rice

Gulab Jamun
SERVES 4

*M*ost Indians have a sweet tooth and like to end their meals with a dessert which is usually milk-based. Gulab jamuns are easy to make with powdered milk and although they are a little on the sweet side, they are a delightful treat.

500ml (16 fl oz) water
250g (8 oz) sugar
4 green cardamoms
$^1/_2$ teaspoon rose essence
60g (2 oz) self-raising flour
1 teaspoon semolina
250g (8 oz) full cream milk
   powder
pinch of saffron, crushed
30g (1 oz) butter
125g (4 oz) paneer,
   (see page 11)
a little warm milk for mixing
   the dough
oil for deep frying

Preparation time: 40 minutes
Cooking time: 20 minutes

1. Put the water, sugar and 2 crushed cardamoms in a pan and place on a medium heat. Boil until the mixture is the consistency of a light syrup. Remove the cardamom skins and leave the syrup to cool. Add the rose essence, cover and set aside.
2. Sieve the flour, semolina, and milk powder into a bowl.
3. Shell the remaining cardamoms, crush the seeds and add to the flour with the saffron. Rub in the butter and crumbled paneer and mix well.
4. Slowly add enough milk to make a soft, smooth and pliable dough. Cover and leave for 30 minutes.
5. Divide the dough into 12 and roll into balls.
6. Put the oil in a kadhai or deep heavy-based pan and place it on a medium heat. Gently and slowly fry the balls until golden brown and thoroughly cooked.
7. Remove the balls with a slotted spoon, shake off any excess oil and put them into the syrup. Place the pan on a medium heat and bring to the boil. Remove the pan from the heat, cover tightly and leave for 3-4 hours for the syrup to be absorbed by the milk balls.

Serve hot or cold as a dessert on their own, or with double cream.

Suitable for freezing.

Rich Rice Pudding
(Kheer)
SERVES 4

*T*his is a traditional Indian rice pudding which is quite different from the Western rice pudding. In Punjab, where dairy products are plentiful, it is very popular.

60g (2 oz) basmati rice
125ml (4 fl oz) water
1 litre (32 fl oz) full cream milk
180g (6 oz) sugar
3 green cardamoms
30g (1 oz) slivered almonds
1 teaspoon rosewater

Preparation time: 15 minutes
Cooking time: 1 hour

1. Wash the rice in several changes of water. Drain well. Add 125ml (4 fl oz) of water and cook in a pan until all the water is absorbed and the rice is soft.
2. Put the milk in a heavy-based pan and bring to the boil. Reduce the heat and add the cooked rice. Simmer on a low heat for about 30 to 45 minutes or until creamy. Stir frequently to prevent the mixture from sticking. Scrape off all the mixture that sticks to the sides of the pan and add to the thickening rice.
3. Add the sugar and stir until dissolved. Remove from the heat.
4. Peel the cardamoms and crush the seeds. Add the cardamom seeds, almonds and rosewater to the pan and mix well. Put in a dish and serve.

Serve hot or cold on its own or to accompany Creamy Pancakes.

Suitable for freezing.

Rich Rice Pudding and Carrot and Milk Pudding (p.148)

Carrot and Milk Pudding
(Gajrela)
SERVES 4

*T*his is one of the choicest sweet dishes of Northern India. In Punjab, it is generally associated with the winter months when a variety of carrots grow profusely. Cooked with milk, sugar, paneer and ghee, 'Gajrela' is a sumptuous dessert.

500ml (16 fl oz) full cream
  milk
500g (1 lb) carrots, scraped and
  finely grated
90g (3 oz) sugar
4 tablespoons ghee
3 green cardamoms
60g (2 oz) paneer, (see page 11)
1 tablespoon slivered almonds
1 tablespoon chopped pistachio
  nuts
1 tablespoon raisins
2-3 silver leaves (optional)

Preparation time: 30 minutes
Cooking time: 45 minutes

1. Put the milk in a deep heavy-based saucepan and place on a high heat. Bring to the boil, lower the heat and add the carrots. Cook until the carrots are soft and most of the liquid has evaporated.
2. Stir in the sugar and cook for 4-5 minutes or until the sugar has dissolved. Stir frequently. Add the ghee and cook for 5-6 minutes.
3. Shell the cardamoms, remove the seeds and grind coarsely. Add to the pan and mix well.
4. Crumble the paneer roughly. Add to the pan and mix thoroughly. Cook for 2-3 minutes. The whole mixture should be fairly dry but moist in texture.
5. Add the almonds, pistachios and raisins. Mix well, cover and remove from the heat. Transfer to a shallow serving dish. Decorate with silver leaves, if liked, and always serve hot.

Serve as a dessert on special occasions.

Suitable for freezing.

Sweet Vermicelli
(*Suki Seviyan*)
SERVES 4

In India, there are very few preparations which call for the use of vermicelli, but this simple dessert is a popular one in Punjab. Traditionally, vermicelli was made at home, but now a variety of vermicelli can be bought. One type is slightly thicker and also comes lightly roasted and is absolutely right for the following recipe.

90g (3 oz) ghee
2 green cardamoms
180g (6 oz) vermicelli
1 tablespoon chopped cashew nuts
1 tablespoon chopped almonds
1 tablespoon sultanas
90g (3 oz) sugar
180ml (6 fl oz) warm water

Preparation time: 15 minutes
Cooking time: 30 minutes

1. Put the ghee in a heavy-based pan and place on a medium heat. Shell the cardamoms, crush the seeds and add to the ghee. Fry for a few seconds.
2. Add the vermicelli and on a low heat, fry until golden brown. This must be done slowly whilst constantly stirring the vermicelli for even browning.
3. Add the cashew nuts, almonds and sultanas and fry for 30-60 seconds.
4. Add the sugar and warm water. Mix gently to avoid breaking up the vermicelli. Cover, and bring to the boil. Reduce the heat and simmer until all the liquid is absorbed and the vermicelli is tender. Be careful not to overcook. Increase the heat and dry off the liquids quickly if the vermicelli looks like being overcooked.

Serve warm sprinkled with soft brown sugar.

Unsuitable for freezing.

Creamy Pancakes
(Malaipura)
SERVES 4

*P*urras are a sweet which are traditionally made during the rainy season in Punjab. Somehow, the dark clouds and the thundering rains that beat down ferociously puts one in a mood to have something nice, warm and filling – and purras are perfect!

150g (5 oz) plain white flour
180ml (6 fl oz) milk
180ml (6 fl oz) double cream
150g (5 oz) sugar
180ml (6 fl oz) water
1/2 teaspoon aniseed, crushed
1/4 teaspoon saffron, crushed
1/2 teaspoon rosewater
oil for shallow frying
2 tablespoons mixed chopped
  nuts

Preparation time: 45 minutes
Cooking time: 20 minutes

1. Put the flour in a bowl. Mix together the milk and cream and add, a little at a time, to the flour. Stir constantly until the mixture becomes a creamy batter of pouring consistency. Add a little more or less liquid as needed. Cover and leave for 30 minutes. Mix well just before use.
2. Put the sugar and water in a pan and place it on a medium heat. Bring to the boil, add the aniseed, lower the heat and simmer until a thick syrup is formed.
3. Remove from the heat, add the saffron and rose-water and set aside.
4. Place a heavy-based frying pan on a medium heat and add enough oil to coat the surface. Pour a tablespoon of batter into the pan and gently swirl it into a circle of about 10cm (4 inches). Lower the heat and fry for about 30 seconds or until the underside is golden brown. Turn over and fry gently for 1 minute or until golden brown. Repeat using the remaining batter to make more pancakes.
5. Arrange the malaipurras on a serving dish, pour the syrup all over and decorate with chopped nuts. Serve hot.

Unsuitable for freezing.

Creamy Pancakes and Mango Ice Cream (p.152)

Mango Ice Cream
(Am di Kulfi)
MAKES 6

*T*his creamy, rich and extravagant dessert is traditionally frozen and served in 'kulfi-de-saanche'. These are small, conical-shaped aluminium moulds that are very inexpensive and available at most Asian supermarkets. A delightful and refreshing change from the usual ice creams, here is a typically Punjabi recipe for mango kulfi.

500g (1 lb) rabhri (see below)
125g (4 oz) fresh mango purée

Preparation time: 15 minutes
Cooking time: 1 hour

1. Put the rabhri in a bowl and when cool add the mango purée. Mix well and fill 6 kulfi moulds or an ice cream mould or foil container and freeze.
2. A few minutes before serving, remove from the freezer and take out of the moulds. If made in one large mould, cut into 2.5cm (1 inch) thick slices.

Serve with slices of fresh mango.

Suitable for freezing.

Rabhri
(Dried Fresh Milk Pudding)

1½ litres (48 fl oz) full cream milk
150g (5 oz) sugar

1. Put the milk in a deep heavy-based pan on a high heat. Bring to the boil, reduce the heat to low and simmer until the milk is reduced to ¼ of its original volume. It is important to stir the milk constantly for the first 15 minutes and then at 2-3 minute intervals. Take care that it does not stick to the base of the pan and does not boil over. Adjust the heat accordingly.
2. When the mixture is creamy, and of a granular-like consistency, add the sugar and stir until dissolved. Remove the pan from the heat. Cool and use as required for Mango Ice Cream.

Ground Rice Pudding
(Phirni)
SERVES 4

A wonderful, creamy ground rice pudding that tastes superb and is also surprisingly simple to make. A common preparation in most Punjabi households, it is traditionally served in earthenware bowls called 'shikoras'.

45g (1½ oz) basmati rice
1 litre (32 fl oz) full cream milk
30g (1 oz) ground cashew nuts, optional
180g (6 oz) sugar
½ teaspoon saffron
1 tablespoon milk
30g (1 oz) slivered almonds
15g (½ oz) shelled pistachios, roughly chopped
1 teaspoon rosewater
4 silver leaves

Preparation time: 30 minutes
Cooking time: 15 minutes

1. Wash the rice in several changes of water, until the water runs clear. Soak in a bowl with sufficient water to cover. Leave for at least 30 minutes.
2. Drain the rice and put it in a liquidizer. Add 1-2 tablespoons of water and process until the rice is ground to a fine paste.
3. In a pan, mix the rice paste with 1 litre (32 fl oz) milk and cook on a medium heat, stirring constantly, until creamy and smooth.
4. Reduce the heat and add the cashew nuts (if used) and sugar. Stir until the mixture begins to thicken.
5. Crush the saffron and mix with 1 tablespoon of milk. Add the saffron and half the almonds and pistachios to the rice. Stir well and remove from the heat and cool.
6. Mix in the rosewater and pour into individual bowls and chill in the fridge until set. Serve decorated with silver leaves and sprinkled with remaining nuts.

Unsuitable for freezing.

Sweets

DRINKS

Apricot Juice

SERVES 6

*D*ue to the abundance of apricots that grow and are harvested in Baltistan, they appear in all forms and varieties. The most common are dried apricots. Try to obtain Hunza apricots from wholefood shops for this recipe. The kernels from the cracked seed are eaten as snacks or used in place of almonds. The sugar used in this recipe is dependent on the sweetness of the original apricot. It is also, however, a preservative for the mixture.

125g (4 oz) dried apricots
125g (4 oz) sugar (omit if not
  required)
600ml (1 pint) water

Preparation: 35 minutes plus soaking time

1. Soak the apricots in boiling water for 30 minutes. If they have stones then remove them.
2. Put the drained apricots and water into a blender and process for 2-3 minutes until well mixed.
3. Transfer to a pan and bring to the boil. Simmer for 10 minutes and add the sugar. Simmer for a further 20 minutes or until mixture thickens.
4. Cool and store in bottles in the refrigerator.

Serve by diluting 4-5 tablespoons in a tall glass with water.

Suitable for freezing.

Previous pages: Apricot Juice, Mint Lassi (p.158) and Almond Juice (p.157)

Almond Juice
SERVES 6-10

This extract is made and stored in the refrigerator. Sometimes a few drops of rose water are added just before serving, to give a rich fragrance. Don't be put off by the amount of sugar added, as this makes a concentrated drink which is later diluted and it is not too sweet.

125g (4 oz) whole almonds
600ml (1 pint) water
4 green cardamom pods
350g (12 oz) sugar

Preparation time: 45 minutes plus soaking time

1. Soak the almonds overnight in water. Drain and discard the water. Peel the almonds and put in a bowl.
2. Peel all the cardamoms and grind the seeds.
3. Add almonds and half the water to a liquidiser and blend into a paste. Add the rest of the water and blend for 3-4 minutes, until all the almonds are well mixed into the water and the mixture is not lumpy.
4. Pour this mixture into a pan, add the sugar and ground cardamoms and bring to the boil. Simmer on low heat for 40 minutes or until the mixture thickens.
5. Cool the mixture and store in a bottle in the refrigerator.

To serve, add 4 tablespoons to a tall glass, top with cold water, add crushed ice-cubes and serve as a cool refreshing drink.

Suitable for freezing.

Drinks

Mint Lassi

SERVES 1-2

4 tablespoons natural yogurt
180ml (6 fl oz) water
6 leaves fresh mint
$^1/_4$ teaspoon salt

1. Put yogurt, water, 3 mint leaves and salt in a blender. Process for 1-2 minutes until frothy.
2. Serve in tall glasses with straws. Garnish with remaining whole mint leaves.

Sweet Lassi

SERVES 1-2

6 tablespoons natural full fat or
   Greek yogurt
90ml (3 fl oz) milk
90ml (3 fl oz) water
2 ice cubes
1 tablespoon sugar
a pinch of salt
60g (2 oz) ripe apple or mango
   (optional)

1. Put all the ingredients into a blender and process for 2-3 minutes until frothy. For a fruity lassi, add the apple or mango and blend with the other ingredients.
2. Serve in tall glasses with straws. Garnish with apple or mango slices.

Salty Lassi

SERVES 1-2

4 tablespoons natural yogurt
180ml (6 fl oz) water
salt to taste
pinch of ground cumin

1. Put all ingredients into a blender and process for 2-3 minutes.
2. Serve in glasses, as an accompaniment to any meal.

Index

Index